The
Craft of the
Warrior

For Patricia,
With your natural
inquisitiveness the way
of the warrior is yours
for the opening.

Robert Spencer

The
Craft of the
Warrior

Robert L. Spencer

North Atlantic Books/Frog, Ltd.
Berkeley, California

Published by
Frog, Ltd.
2800 Woolsey St.
Berkeley, California 94705

Frog, Ltd. books are distributed by
North Atlantic Books
P.O. Box 12327
Berkeley, California 94701

Cover and book design by Paula Morrison
Typeset by Catherine Campaigne

The terms *Feldenkrais*®, *Feldenkrais*® *Method,*
Awareness Through Movement®, and *Functional Integration*®
are registered service marks of The Feldenkrais Guild.

First Frog, Ltd. publication 1993

Library of Congress Cataloging-in-Publication Data

Spencer, Robert L., 1947–
   The craft of the warrior / Robert L. Spencer.
     p. cm.
   Includes biographical references and index.
   ISBN 1-883319-05-6
   1. Self-actualization (Psychology) I. Title.
BF637.S4S67   1993   93–8530
158'.1—dc20   CIP

    1   2   3   4   5   6   7   8   9   /   97   96   95   94   93

To Faye—my wife, partner, and magical companion.

Acknowledgments

Many thanks to those who have taught, counseled, and supported me in learning what was necessary to write this book. Dr. Robert Lehman and Colleen Buchanan helped edit the first draft and kept my thinking straight. Thanks also to Sal Glynn and Kathy Glass at North Atlantic Books. They made the editing process educational rather than tedious while shaping the final form of the book.

I have had too many profound teachers to mention them all, but they include my family, my colleagues, my friends, and my students over the years.

Particularly formative have been these teachers:

Brook Medicine Eagle, who introduced me to The *Feldenkrais*® Method, Neuro-Linguistic Programming, and Shamanism, all on the same day.

Dennis Leri and Mark Reese, Feldenkrais Trainers who profoundly influenced my ability to move, feel, and think more fluidly and with greater precision.

Moshe Feldenkrais and Milton Erickson, neither of whom I met in their lifetimes, but whose influence is with me constantly.

Contents

Introduction

THERE IS A story in theatrical circles about a young English actor who was studying his script while riding on a city bus. An older actor noticed this and told the young man never to prepare in public. He said that if people knew how actors prepared and produced their craft they would lose their sense of magic. Without the magic, what appeal would the theater hold?

This is one way of looking at the magic. But for some people, delving into the "how" of a craft heightens their sense of, and appreciation for, the magic. For them, understanding the workings of the craft reveals its magical nature. This book is written for those people.

This book is about the craft of the warrior. It is about the mystery of the nuts and bolts of the mystery. When you are initiated into a mystery, you are allowed to see the secrets. Prior to initiation, you can only marvel at the appearance. The mystery is designed to keep you mystified. Initiation introduces you to the craft behind the mystery and allows you to participate in its formation and continuation. It also mystifies you about the next level of the mystery, building your desire for the next degree of initiation.

Reading a book cannot substitute for an initiation, but it can take you beyond a certain level of mystification. It can give you a direction and context for further exploration. It can provide a frame of reference.

Knowledge is available in three domains:

1. The exoteric. This is the beginning level. It is like being in the audience, which is a step closer to knowledge about the play than being on the street.
2. The mesoteric. This is a level of admission to theory and basic practices. It is like taking a class about acting.

3. The esoteric. This is the level of initiation into the inner practices. It is the actual acting, often involving the guidance of a mentor or group.

The frame of reference for this book is what I call "public domain warriorship." The sources are reasonably available for anyone with a requisite amount of determination to find them. Sometimes all that is required is to go to your bookstore and then commit the time necessary to read the source material. Sometimes this goes quickly and sometimes you must plow through the books sentence by sentence or word by word. Another level of commitment is required if you want to participate in training for a craft, either as a vocation or avocation, that provides a continuing vehicle for growth and a form for personal discipline. Training in such methods requires a commitment of time, energy, and money, but it is readily available to the public. There are some sources discussed in this book that require more effort to locate, but they can be found if you are determined. These groups are semi-secretive, and you will have to demonstrate your sincere interest to gain admission. However the ideas presented here can be followed by anyone who wants to do so. You do not have to leave the country, quit your job, or join some exotic sect to benefit from them. In fact, the purpose of this book is to provide a frame of reference sufficient for the reader to begin the practice of warriorship at the mesoteric level.

This book, by itself, will not take you across the threshold. But it will show you that there are doors where you might not have seen them before. With this information you can develop both the skill and perspective to open them. By applying what you learn from this book, you can gain enough personal power to cross the threshold and explore what lies beyond the doorway. Perhaps you will find the doorway that opens to your own path with heart.

In this book a warrior is defined as "an impeccable hunter of personal power." The quest for personal power is a quest for evolution, not for domination. It is a quest designed to bring you face to face with your magnificence. You will discover barriers to manifesting this magnificence, and you will find that you need to change your mind. These are not limitations. They are problems you can solve. This is a guidebook for finding solutions, and it presupposes that human improvement can continue infinitely.

The material in this book is intended to serve men and women equally, as warriorship is not gender specific. You will find that I have alternated masculine and feminine pronouns, using the masculine in one chapter and the feminine in the next, unless the reference is to a specific person. I chose this way to give equal representation without impairing the flow of reading.

The book will connect you with authors, teachers and sources who have travelled the warrior's way before you. Let the perspectives you gain from this book guide you in choosing your routes of further exploration. I offer it for your benefit and to promote the welfare of all our relations on this beautiful planet.

Chapter One

The Emerging Myth

MYTHS DEFINE OUR possibilities. As archetypes, mythic figures represent the qualities and potentials inherent in us all. The actual stories and legends are vehicles for expressing these qualities, and the glamorous, adventuresome nature of myths captures the attention of the parts of our psyches that relate to symbolism. Psychologist and psycho-historian Jean Houston refers to myths as the DNA of the psyche, containing the "genetic code" of our psychic constitution. The stories are told and retold, heard and reheard, and the special aspects of our conscious or unconscious nature relate to the symbolic characters and events in the myth, giving us a fuller, richer picture of ourselves and our relationship with the universe around us. So it is with the myth of the warrior—a myth that is reforming itself from the ancient warrior codes into stories and practices befitting current times and people.

Stories and legends have always been told of those who lived more fully than the rest of us, and of those who had knowledge, powers, or attributes beyond the everyday world where ordinary people are confined. The bravery of those special ones has been admired greatly, as has their dedication to their quest and discipline. Odysseus, Merlin, Moses, Miyamoto, Nasrudin—the names leap out from many cultures, with each hero exemplifying dedication to an ideal and the discipline required to travel a chosen path. They all possess something extraordinary, be it physical strength, secret knowledge, a compelling vision, or special guidance from the gods. Through these mythic figures we are given glimpses of the possible and assurance that there is more to life and more to the world than what we encounter in seemingly ordinary existence. The heroes and warriors of the myths represent the archetypes of our own inner workings. Odysseus' journey signifies our own; each spell cast by Merlin whispers that we all have powers yet untapped; each story of the Mullah Nasrudin draws us to our own deeper wisdom.

If the mythic figures highlight our possibilities, what is to be said for our daily lives in the ordinary world? Our Western culture, with its focus on rationality and mechanization, has lost much of the richness of ourselves conveyed in myth. In fact, the word "myth" is often used to denigrate and trivialize a belief, dismissing it as fiction, as a myth to be "exploded," showing it to be an unscientific, misleading farce. Dismissing the myths, we resign ourselves to the "real world," assigning those grand adventures, along with all they could mean to us personally and collectively, to the realm of fantasy. No wonder we characterize ourselves as struggling in the rat race, finding our time, energy, and ambition absorbed in the struggle for the legal tender. The parts of our lives not dedicated to earning money for survival become focused on such "real world" issues as status, fashion, material acquisition, political or religious dominance, and the pursuit of leisure. In the face of the massive efforts we make in these pursuits, our sensitivities become diminished and finally we can only respond to gross forms of stimulation. Soon drugs, horror movies, and an obsession with the negative events around us permeate our culture. We search for guidance and a code of living, but usually find more of the same, with boredom, depression, fear, and alienation the results.

The discontents of civilization, however, prove that the longing within us is still alive. The rat race and gross levels of stimulation offered as entertainment can be seen as ways of trying to get beyond the confines of the material web that entangles us. Even though that strategy does not work, there is an assertion in the struggle that there must be something more to life. Our definition of the "real world" inhibits us from embracing the archetypal realm exemplified in legend and myth, and the unmet desire for the "more" erupts into excess and violence.

This is not surprising, after all, in a culture that loses the teaching stories that guide its members, provide a basis for right living, and hint at the levels of knowledge possible. The separation and alienation we feel from the rest of the universe is the price we pay. The rampant materialism and disregard for others and for the environmental resources upon which we depend have replaced the feeling of being a part of the world and knowing our place in the scheme of things. This loss is felt deeply by countless people, many of whom cannot identify what it is they are missing and who are not quite sure from what it is they are alienated. They just know that there must be *more*.

Yet our connections to our mythic roots are not completely severed. Many of the old stories still survive in one form or another, and many people have turned their search for context and meaning outside the cultural mainstream. There has been a rapidly developing interest in Oriental martial arts and the warrior cultures that produced those arts. Thousands of people are adopting and appreciating Native American traditions, which also have strong warrior codes.

In the midst not only of longing and disillusionment, but of this widespread search for the truth, a new myth is emerging. There is a body of tales and teachings surfacing to serve as a guide, as a psychic road map of the routes to a rich sense of connection and purpose. The ancient warrior traditions, indigenous to every continent's history, are receiving a revival and renovation so that they apply to the present. The new legends provide a code to the universe that can be used by modern people who must deal with today's society. Those who decipher the code will claim a new relationship to the world—a relationship that provides context, orientation, and purpose. This code guides us in relating to all things, understanding our place in the order of the world, and developing a wider and deeper perspective; enhancing our perception, sensitivity and action; exercising free choice within the parameters of personal discipline; and living healthy physical, mental, emotional, and spiritual lives. Emerging in the tales and writings of the last half century, and supported by teachings far older, is the new warrior mythology.

Myths are the substance of subjective history. It is useless to evaluate them in terms of objective history because their value does not lie in the establishing of facts, but in the capturing of subjective experience. The value of the myth is that it serves as a guidebook around which people can orient their experiences and set their directions. The factual precision of the stories that set forth the myth is beside the point. The warriors and warrior apprentices personify the struggle to gain a way of relating to an infinitely complex universe and the inexplicable forces it contains. These characters show us the frustrating limits of rationality and our habitual patterns of acting, thinking, feeling, and sensing. The warriors show us alternatives that make life purposeful, enjoyable, and connected to the patterns around us. The warrior myth says that we all have the potential to live according to the warrior's code and to use the warrior's framework for choosing our actions and perceptions.

The Sources

The warriorship literature contains both fiction and non-fiction. The line is sometimes difficult to distinguish, but it is not particularly important to do so if you keep in mind that what is developing here is a mythology. Whether objective or subjective, there is always a component of reality in history. As we will see later, there is also great difficulty in trying to establish what reality is exactly. If we decide to approach all the sources of the warriorship literature with the intention of extracting the important teachings that have to do with the code of living like a warrior, it is not necessary to draw strict boundaries on validity based on either subjectivity or objectivity. Much of the time the fictional and non-fictional sources corroborate each other and address the same issues. Throughout this book we will venture to find the commonalities in the sources and to distill an understanding of the often elusive points of warriorship.

Castaneda
The works of Carlos Castaneda form a cornerstone of the modern warrior myth. To date Castaneda has written eight books about his

experiences over more than two decades with a Yaqui Indian warrior and teacher, don Juan. Readers sometimes question the authenticity of Castaneda's tales, but the objective authenticity is not the issue here. As with all myths, the value of the warrior myth does not lie in objective occurrence. Castaneda and his characters resonate with our psyches, and the widespread popularity of his books shows that many people relate to what he offers.

Castaneda's books began with *The Teachings of Don Juan: A Yaqui Way of Knowledge,* published in 1968. Castaneda describes himself as a self-assured graduate student in anthropology at U.C.L.A. who ventures into the Sonoran Desert in Arizona in search of someone who could give him information about hallucinogenic plants used in Indian rituals and healing practices. He found such a man, and much more. Don Juan Matus, no doubt a fictional name, is a Yaqui Indian who is a *brujo,* or sorcerer. Don Juan's presence exerts a strange effect on young Carlos. While still thinking he is going to learn about desert plants for his dissertation, Carlos becomes an apprentice to don Juan, who grooms him to become a *man of knowledge.* Carlos' training lasted for many years, but don Juan insisted almost from the beginning that if Carlos was to survive the experiences with the unknown and muster the necessary discipline he would have to learn to live like a warrior. The system of knowledge Carlos was to learn would strain his rationality and physical resources severely and require a new way of life. To successfully negotiate this challenging course of learning, Carlos had to grasp the warrior's way, for as don Juan said, "The frightening nature of knowledge leaves one no alternative but to become a warrior."[1]

Castaneda's trials in learning the sorcerer's way of knowledge under don Juan and another primary teacher, don Genaro, fill the first four books of his series. Throughout these books the basic requirements of warriorship are presented to Carlos, and his teachers demand that he learn to live in that way. His attempts to learn the warrior's way are fraught with the same difficulties, resistances, elusive moments of understanding, frustration, doubts, and exhilaration that would characterize any of us in attempting such a task. At no time does Carlos offer himself to us as a prize pupil or metaphysical genius. The warrior's way for him is truly a struggle and challenge, and the barriers he must overcome are the same any of us could expect to face. At the end of *Tales of Power,* Castaneda finishes his apprenticeship and must continue on his path without don Juan, which is exactly what he does in *The Second Ring of Power.*

Later, in *The Eagle's Gift,* Castaneda begins a process of recollecting a parallel series of adventures that he experienced contiguously with those in the first four books, but in a different state called *heightened awareness.* Only by integrating the learning from both realms could he accomplish his task of becoming a man of knowledge. These recollections are from Carlos' personal experiences and from stories don Juan told him about his own apprenticeship. So far, the last book in the series is *The Power of Silence,* published in 1987, but there is plenty of material for future books.

Castaneda's books teach about warriorship in both lecture and experiential format. Don Juan would tutor Carlos for hours in terms of theory and some point of living like a warrior. Then he would lead or send Carlos on an adventure to take the abstract point and make it real. Carlos delivers his experiences in the deserts and mountains of Mexico in the age-old format of teaching stories, in which many readings are necessary to get the learning value. Each encounter with a story, especially after one has had more experience with the whole series of books, yields more information and makes the often-bizarre tales more relevant. Carlos' adventures usually take place in remote locales, but they symbolize the confrontations with limitations that any of us who aspire to become warriors must overcome, whether we do so in the desert or city.

It is not possible for me to recreate here the rich tales of adventure told by Castaneda. We will gain a conceptual understanding of warriorship and many of its principles, but the reader should explore the works of Castaneda and the writers of the other sources described to capture the richness of the teaching. Even extensive reading of the literature, however, will produce only an inferior form of understanding unless you find applications in yourself and your life for the ideas Castaneda offers you.

Millman

Between 1979 and 1992 Dan Millman published four books used as references here, in addition to two children's books about warriorship. Two of four books discussed here are novels—*Way of the Peaceful Warrior* and *Sacred Journey of the Peaceful Warrior*. Millman makes this clear in the preface to *Way of the Peaceful Warrior*, but adds that much of the book is autobiographical material enhanced with metaphors and anecdotes to highlight the main teaching points.

Way of the Peaceful Warrior has definite parallels to Castaneda's books, as Millman weaves a tale of how, as a university student, he meets an old warrior he calls Socrates and begins an apprenticeship with him. Like don Juan, Socrates is able to perform unbelievable feats and seems to manifest powers beyond the merely human. Socrates is also a model of impeccability, as he has overcome his habits and does not waste his power on trivial pursuits such as establishing his own importance or avoiding his weaknesses. Like Carlos, Millman is a bungling apprentice, making all the mistakes you and I would probably make. He has flashes of insight and ability, glimpses of the *more* that exists beyond his previous ideas about life; but, alas, all too often these are just flashes, impossible to maintain. Through all his ups and downs, including an extended time when, like Castaneda, Millman quit the entire business of becoming a warrior, the lure of what could be proves too powerful to resist and he always returns to the way. *Way of the Peaceful Warrior* is a good introductory work to the warriorship literature. Since most of Millman's early adventures took place in Berkeley, California, rather than the Sonoran Desert, the reader copes more with changing internal landscapes than external ones.

Sacred Journey of the Peaceful Warrior continues the autobiographical/mythical story of Dan Millman after the time of Socrates. Millman has hit the low point in his life and sets out to travel the world to find some way to put himself back together again. Even though he is out of shape spiritually, his old training serves him well enough to discover his next main teacher, Mama Chia. Mama Chia is a shaman in Hawaii and, like Socrates, a fictionalized and enhanced character from Millman's real life. These teachers are probably composite characters, a blend of elements from some of Millman's real teachers (an impressive list given in the Acknowledgments of *Way of the Peaceful Warrior*) and characteristics or knowledge gained through his experiences. This is a well-established formula for passing along mythical wisdom in story form. In *Sacred Journey of the Peaceful Warrior*, Millman presents the basis for a self-development program that he offers in great specificity in a later book. With Mama Chia's help he learns to balance body, mind, and spirit in a way that lets him live a harmonious life, minimizing obstructions to the flow of life force. This is Millman's program for developing impeccability.

In his non-fiction books, *The Warrior Athlete* and *No Ordinary Moments*, Millman offers ways of clearing obstructions, either mental, physical, or spiritual, so that a warrior can live a life of health, power, and effectiveness.

The Warrior Athlete is designed to help the reader prepare for excellent levels of performance. Although athletic performance is the primary arena of the book, the material applies to any endeavor. Millman supplies illustrative exercises and experiences to clarify his theoretical points. In developing his theory, Millman gives the reader a beautiful philosophical model for relating self-development to anything you need to do in life. He describes the roles of preparation, awareness, meditation, whole-self integration, and other important concepts in building one's abilities to perform in life's arenas. All in all, the book does an excellent job of taking many of the abstract principles of warriorship and, through the metaphor of athletics, making them concrete.

The title of *No Ordinary Moments*, the latest book of the series, comes from an incident in *Way of the Peaceful Warrior*. It is an apt title, for Millman believes, as do the other sources in the warrior mythology, that wasting time and energy is antithetical to one's well-being. The phrase "no ordinary moments" means that all of life is important and deserves one's full presence and attention.

In this book, Millman details the theory and practices of the program he learned from Mama Chia and Socrates. He explains that human beings have three selves: the Basic Self, that comprises the body and subconscious processes; the Conscious Self, composed of the intellect, reason, and ego; and the Higher Self, one's spiritual nature. Millman's model of human functioning proposes that each person receives a supply of universal energy that is supposed to flow freely through him, yielding the ability to live up to his potential for performance and happiness. However, if we have physical or mental obstructions, accumulations of this energy are uncomfortable and we seek to discharge it in many ways—some productively, some damaging. Millman's program offers advice on two levels. The first is to substitute productive forms of energy discharge for damaging ones (although both constitute addictions in his model). The second level is to use his practices to clear the obstructions, which lead one to walk the way of the peaceful warrior.

Shambhala

Shambhala is a mythical kingdom in Tibet, whose rulers and people manifest the qualities of warriorship and wisdom handed down through generations. There are stories of such a kingdom in many Oriental societies, setting forth a body of teaching that composes part of the foundation of Eastern religion and thought concerning the nature of the world and human beings. Chögyam Trungpa, a Tibetan Buddhist Rinpoche, has brought the story of Shambhala to the West in the book *Shambhala, The Sacred Path of the Warrior* and by offering a variety of Shambhala training programs. He differentiates this material from Buddhist religious training, preferring to characterize this path of warriorship as "secular enlightenment."

There are many ways to think of the kingdom of Shambhala. Some contend that it was an historical, ancient kingdom in Central Asia. Others believe it still exists in some remote mountain location. Other legends say that because of the degree of enlightenment of its citizens, the entire kingdom departed to a more celestial realm. Trungpa reinforces the value of myth, as he writes, "It is not important to determine whether the kingdom of Shambhala is fact or fiction. Instead, we should appreciate and emulate the ideal of an enlightened society that it represents."[2]

Trungpa's book addresses many of the tenets of warriorship from a different perspective that, whether he calls it religious or secular, is deeply influenced by Buddhism. There is a gentleness and vulnerability to Trungpa's warriors that bring the ideals of compassion and love into the arena of fearlessness. He describes how the warrior comes to accept the basic goodness that is, finally, the nature of the world and oneself. Trungpa describes the discipline of sitting meditation and delineates its place in the personal development of warriors. Although *Shambhala* is a small book, it is densely packed with information and offers a thorough treatise on what Trungpa calls "the sacred path of the warrior."

Nuclear physicist Jeremy Hayward combines Trungpa's teachings with ideas from Western biology and physics in a book called *Perceiving Ordinary Magic: Science and Intuitive Wisdom.* Hayward was a senior student of Trungpa's and has been involved extensively with the Naropa Institute and Shambhala Training in Colorado. In the book Hayward correlates many Buddhist ideas on perception, awareness, and belief systems with theories and findings of Western science. He follows the intuitive ways of knowing that stem from meditation and compares them with the rational way of finding things out used in science.

The Fourth Way

G. I. Gurdjieff was an astonishing character. Born in Alexandropol in one of the remote provinces of what became the U.S.S.R., he decided at an early age to dedicate his life to answering the question, "What is the sense and significance of life on earth and human life in particular?" When he was eight years old, his grandmother on her deathbed called young Gurdjieff to her side and told him, "Never do as others do." It was advice he was to follow all his life as he set out to answer his prime question.

Gurdjieff and his followers believed there is an ancient body of knowledge, originally transmitted from sources of intelligence higher than mankind, that holds the truth about the way the universe works. Gurdjieff worked from the premise that this knowledge existed in his time, the late nineteenth and early twentieth centuries, in isolated locations, guarded by individuals or groups that had received the teachings from a long lineage of masters of wisdom. The tales of Gurdjieff's search for these mysterious people and knowledge are fascinating, as are the stories of how he attempted to bring the knowledge he found to the West.

The Institute for the Harmonious Development of Man was founded first in Moscow and finally in Paris. Gurdjieff travelled from there to lecture and teach in other parts of the world, and to confer with some of his students and associates who were attempting to spread the word. He developed what became known as The Fourth Way schools, dedicated to spreading the knowledge and practices Gurdjieff's group had learned to help Western people wake up and develop their consciousness.

In addition, Gurdjieff wrote three series of books, "modestly" titled *All and Everything. Beelzebub's Tales to His Grandson* was the first series. Gurdjieff also titled this series *An Objectively Impartial Criticism of the Life of Man.* According to Gurdjieff the purpose of the first series of books is "to destroy, mercilessly, without any compromises whatsoever, in the mentation and feeling of the reader, the beliefs and views, by centuries rooted in him, about everything existing in the world."[3] In *Beelzebub's Tales* Gurdjieff lays out the basis for the human condition and offers an incredibly complex cosmology of how the universe is structured and operates. It is difficult reading, and he recommends reading these books three times, with escalating degrees of intensity. Gurdjieff claimed that he delineated many of the truths he discovered in this three-volume series, but he often offered them in *legominisms,* which means they are draped in metaphor and coded in often obscure language, frequently requiring much research in order to understand a single word. Gurdjieff apparently thought one should have access to the truth but should have to earn it and do much preparation to be ready for it.

Gurdjieff later wrote *Meetings with Remarkable Men,* which can be read on several levels ranging from a travelogue to a treatise on esoteric wisdom. Although published as a single volume, Gurdjieff thought of this as a series of three books. He wrote that the purpose of this series was "to acquaint the reader with the material required for a new creation and to prove the soundness and good quality of it."[4] In this book Gurdjieff describes many of the profound teachers he encountered, beginning with his own father. It is much easier reading than *Beelzebub's Tales*.

The third series, which was not generally available until the last few years, is called *Life Is Real Only Then, When "I Am."* Gurdjieff intended this to be a series of four books whose purpose was "to assist the arising, in the mentation and in the feelings of the reader, of a veritable, nonfantastic representation not of that illusory world which he now perceives, but of the world existing in reality."[5] These writings were intended for advanced students in the Fourth Way; however, Gurdjieff never finished this work. The single volume available today is a fragmentary work that ends in mid-sentence. There is some interesting material from Gurdjieff's life including stories of the three times he was hit by stray bullets and the tales of his recovery and what he learned from the experiences. He also describes the decision process behind his writing. Most of the book, however, relates to his visits to the United States and includes some of the lectures and exercises he gave to his group of American students.

Gurdjieff's success as a writer is dubious. His writing is obscured by incredibly long sentences and the cloaking of his meaning in mysterious language. To understand the value, the reader must commit to multiple, in-depth readings of the material, with many pauses to reflect on the meaning of the sentences. It is often like doing literary archaeology, carefully brushing aside the verbal dust to find the priceless artifact buried beneath. With his writing Gurdjieff wanted to reach many more people than he could teach personally. He planed to shake up their existing world view with *Beelzebub's Tales*, establish the foundation for an alternate description of reality with *Meetings with Remarkable Men*, and then fill the gap with *Life Is Real Only Then, When "I Am."* If the reader can sift through the first series, he will certainly find his ideas on possible cosmologies loosened. Reading the second series is like looking through windows of lost civilizations. The third series was only partially completed, and its value is correspondingly diminished.

The Fourth Way is the particular path of personal development taught by Gurdjieff and his associates based on the knowledge they gained of the ancient truths and practices. In contrast to the first three ways—the way of the Monk, the way of the Yogi, and the way of the Fakir—the Fourth Way does not require a withdrawal from the world around us. It is designed to release its followers from the "prison" of the ordinary world while still interacting with it. Although the Fourth Way students and teachers did not refer to themselves as warriors, many of their ideas and practices not only coincide with the other sources on warriorship, but they provide a great deal of practical and theoretical guidance. The writings on the Fourth Way form an integral part of the literature available to direct those who seek the warrior's path.

Several other authors supplemented Gurdjieff's writing and teaching. The ones most often used as sources for this book are P. D. Ouspensky and J. G. Bennett. Ouspensky, who many believe was one of Gurdjieff's best pupils, was also an outstanding individual thinker who added his own ideas to the Fourth Way teachings. Of his several important books, *The Fourth Way* is of particular relevance to our purposes here. The cover of the book describes its contents as "a lucid explanation of the practical side of G. I. Gurdjieff's teachings." It is a verbatim transcript of Ouspensky's lectures to his students from 1921 to 1946, containing very detailed descriptions of many of the ideas encountered in the warriorship literature.

J. G. Bennett was a highly prolific writer. He based his works not only on what he learned from Gurdjieff, but from many other sources as well. Bennett was a traveler, seeker, and scholar in his own right, and his investigations traced the wisdom Gurdjieff referred to from ancient times to modern ones. Bennett also had a following of pupils, and his writings contain some of the exercises and practices they were assigned for their own development.

In 1986 American psychologist Charles Tart published *Waking Up: Overcoming the Obstacles to Human Potential.* This book offers an updated psychological interpretation of many of the concepts and practices of The Fourth Way schools. It is written in an understandable way and draws from information that may be more familiar to contemporary audiences than some of the other works described in this section. For the reader who begins with *Waking Up,* I recommend reading some of the works of Gurdjieff or Ouspensky also. In using the psychological metaphor to interpret such difficult-to-understand ideas as identification and self-remembering, Tart avoided some of the more esoteric meanings, possibly leaving an incomplete picture. Tart's book provides a valuable service even so, because he constructs a starting place for understanding that which often defies explanation.

The link between warriorship and the Fourth Way was forged by Robert deRopp, a student of Ouspensky's, in the book *The Warrior's Way, The Challenging Life Games.* Throughout this essentially auto-biographical work, deRopp relates his experiences with people he considers warriors. In this regard it is much like Gurdjieff's *Meetings with Remarkable Men,* as deRopp describes what he learned from these interesting people—like Gurdjieff, Ouspensky, Bennett, Alan Watts, Charles Lindberg, and others—and what they were like. After studying the works of many of those people I enjoyed reading about their personal lives. DeRopp is not shy about revealing their weaknesses and issues of personal challenge, while he also toasts their strengths and exceptional abilities.

Feldenkrais

More than an author of books, Moshe Feldenkrais was a pioneer in finding ways of improving human functioning. An Israeli nuclear physicist, Feldenkrais and his work are only now starting to enjoy widespread recognition in North America and Europe. Feldenkrais generated a method of overcoming limitations by an organically based process of building personal awareness of how actions are accomplished, and inducing change in a way acceptable to a person's system of self-organization. In many ways the process parallels how people grow from infancy to adulthood, or at least how they would mature if caretakers promoted the natural course of learning rather than interfering with it.

Feldenkrais began his work as a way of coping with a severe knee injury which, in the 1930s, could not be repaired surgically. Calling upon his knowledge of physics, engineering, and martial arts, he was determined to find a way to learn to do the things he needed and wanted to do again. When his base of knowledge proved too limited, he expanded his search into physiology, psychiatry, biology, and other academic areas, as well as non-traditional methods such as F. M. Alexander's work. To make a long story short, Feldenkrais was so successful that he was able to become the first European to hold a black belt in judo, and he never had surgery on his knee. Born in Russia and later immigrating to Palestine, France and England, he arrived in the new nation of Israel after World War II. Feldenkrais continued to explore and expand his new method, eventually dedicating himself to it full-time. In 1969 he trained a handful of practitioners of his method in Israel. In 1977 in San Francisco the first group of trainees outside Israel graduated. Since that time several hundred more practitioners of the Feldenkrais Method have been, and are being, trained in North America, Australia, Europe, and Israel.

In training to become Feldenkrais practitioners, students are exposed to many of the ideas and practices from the other warriorship sources already described. To be sure, the training is not couched in these terms, but the concordance of ideas and the way of viewing the process of actualizing human potential are similar. This form of training is oriented toward teaching people ways to overcome limitations, not in prescribed patterns, but by letting their most natural processes unfold. This requires practitioners to enter the unknown as they work in order to help their pupils (not patients) find the self-knowledge needed to improve. Without the refuge of knowing a prescribed procedure for a known diagnosis, the practitioner must cultivate a warrior's spirit in order to work.

There are many times in this book when Feldenkrais' material is used to establish or illustrate a point regarding warriorship. Feldenkrais wrote several books about his theories, some of which contain actual lessons for learning to improve one's actions. The basis of this process is movement, since movement is necessary for any accomplishment, no matter how physical, intellectual, or artistic it seems. However, Feldenkrais clearly establishes that any human activity involves acting, thinking, sensing, and feeling all working together to produce effectiveness. When one part does not work with the others, as is usually the case to one degree or another, the functioning becomes disintegrated.

Feldenkrais' books are not the only source material used here. There is a great deal of his teaching on audio or videotape, some of which is available to the public directly. Much of this teaching, however, is available through his practitioners' work with the public in the forms of classes, workshops, and individual sessions.

One of the Feldenkrais practitioners who articulates the method's relationship to the warrior's way is Dennis Leri, who has also practiced martial arts for more than twenty years. Leri has written about warriorship in an article in *The Feldenkrais Journal* entitled "Dreams in the Warrior's Wake" (1986, Number Two, 36, 37). As one of only a few senior practitioners authorized to train new practitioners, Leri incorporates his ideas on warriorship into his teaching. Some examples are offered in later chapters.

A Course In Miracles

Offered by the Foundation for Inner Peace, *A Course In Miracles* is an impressive adjunct to the warriorship literature. This is a three-volume work which includes a text, workbook, and manual for teachers. The workbook has 365 daily lessons, and if one follows the instructions, the practice can have a profound effect. The Course is much more religiously oriented than the other sources of the warrior teachings, but the student has a great deal of freedom to interpret the words. One can substitute the word Love for the word God without losing any of the message.

The Course makes its main contributions to warriorship practice in the way it defines and treats the notions of fear and ego. As we will see later, cultivating fearlessness and eliminating self-importance are two of the primary endeavors for warriors. The perspective of the Course, combined with the daily exercises, can be valuable aids in letting go of fear and learning to differentiate between one's true essence and the acquired self-image known as the ego.

Neuro-Linguistic Programming

In the mid-1970s a powerful new way of understanding people's thought processes, emotions, and choices came upon the scene. Developed by mathematician Richard Bandler and linguist John Grinder, it was called Neuro-Linguistic Programming, or NLP. These two developed a way of detecting, analyzing, and using the components of subjective experience that illumine how people experience reality, form beliefs, generate emotions, and produce actions. Applications of NLP include communications, organizational development, psychotherapy, family and relationship counseling, business practices, interpersonal negotiation, performance enhancement, and cross-cultural explorations. Since the inception of NLP, Bandler and Grinder have been joined by many others who have helped to expand the NLP technology into diverse areas of human interest. Besides the works of the founders, we will draw upon the teachings of other NLP practitioners, specifically Leslie Cameron-Bandler, Michael Lebeau, and Nelson Zink.

One of the presuppositions of NLP that is most relevant to this book came from Alfred Korzybsky, a much earlier student of communication: "The map is not the territory."[6] This sentence, more than any other, describes the warrior's epistomology (a theory of the nature and grounds of knowledge). NLP has studied the ways in which people organize their thought processes and determine what they think is real. It turns out that we adopt certain ways of perceiving, based on experience and beliefs, that determine what kinds of sensory stimuli we allow into awareness. Essentially, we interpret our sensory data through the filters of our beliefs and experiences. If we do not believe in something, chances are we will not perceive it. If we perceive it, we will interpret it in a way that is consistent with our structure of beliefs. Because each one of us has a unique background, we have unique realities. Other warrior exponents have similar views even though they use different words to explain them.

NLP is, in essence, a process of modelling, or describing and utilizing maps. One of the main applications has been to model the inner processes of people who are excellent in some field, say, psychotherapy or business. By understanding how these people arrange their maps of reality, including the inner strategies they use, NLP practitioners can build a model of the person's functioning and teach it to others. If the others are able to produce similarly effective results, the model is deemed accurate. From this process have come most of the specific techniques of NLP. For example, a man who had cured himself of a phobia was modelled and his model taught to others. Many of these people have been able to rid themselves of their phobia in a matter of minutes. With earlier forms of psychotherapy it usually takes months or years.

With NLP it is possible to determine the inner strategies people use to make decisions, motivate themselves, learn, and organize themselves for performance. These processes are usually so habituated and unconscious that the person has little awareness of what happens inside. When questioned they say, "I don't know how I do it—I just do it!" With NLP the strategy can be elicited piece by piece, and it becomes evident where the strategy is effective and where it has trouble. If desired, it can be altered so the person functions and feels better.

NLP represents the state of the art in determining the fundamental components of experience. If psychology showed us that atoms compose matter, NLP shows us the sub-atomic particles.

This book draws on several NLP books. Judith DeLozier and John Grinder have published *Turtles All the Way Down,* which is a transcript of a workshop called "Prerequisites to Personal Genius." It borrows in places from Castaneda and approaches some of his ideas from the NLP perspective. In addition, Grinder and DeLozier give specific methods of altering states of personal organization in order to maximize creativity and action. Leslie Cameron-Bandler and Michael Lebeau's book *The Emotional Hostage* provides a framework and practices for using one's emotions in a productive way and introduces practical ways for making choices about emotional states.

In a different category is Nelson Zink's *The Structure of Delight.* This book is a collection of teaching stories about a wise old man named Noom, his somewhat unwilling apprentice Jay, and various other characters from their lives, including a highly evolved mule named Boondoggle. Noom describes a worldwide network of people called the Hawkeen, who easily fit our criteria as warriors. There is no doubt that Zink is referring to a collection of NLP practitioners, or like-minded people. Embedded in the book are many of the NLP viewpoints and processes in allegory form. It is a magnificent way to present the work.

Nowhere in Dan Millman's works does he make reference to NLP or being familiar with it. Still, many of the exercises in *No Ordinary*

Moments have a distinctly NLP flavor. Either Millman is familiar with it, or both sources approach human change work from similar bases.

Other Sources

Once you begin to look for ways and means in which the modern warrior myth is emerging, you find it in many places. Seldom is it mentioned directly, but you can find explanations of the principles in scientific writings, religious teaching, even movies. There will be several of these sources used in the following pages, and it is often surprising to find the many ways in which the warrior myth appears, even when the author probably never thought about applying the word "warrior" to his or her work.

Books are not the only way to learn about the warrior's way. There are also workshops, schools, and conferences. Dan Millman offers Peaceful Warrior Training Seminars, and many Shambhala Training Centers exist in North America and Europe. Information on these opportunities is given in the Appendix. There are also Gurdjieff/Ouspensky institutes and programs at various locations around the country, although they are often semi-secretive and take some effort to locate. Charles Tart gives advice in an appendix of *Waking Up* on finding a Gurdjieff group, and he also offers sound advice on both the benefits and possible pitfalls of group work.

That so many sources exist defining, supporting, or explaining the principles harvested for this book is evidence that something is afoot. At a time when it is sorely needed by people learning to cope with the complex conditions of today's world, a code of living and growing is emerging. For those not satisfied to live according to the consensus trance that passes as ordinary existence, for those that know there must be something *more*, the myth of the warrior is resurfacing. As Gurdjieff might have said, for those with eyes to see, let them see; and for those with ears to hear, let them hear.

Chapter Two

The Path with Heart

IN THIS CHAPTER we will talk about what it means to be a warrior and how one's life and character change when the warrior's path is taken. Not everyone will have the gumption to take it. The warrior's path is demanding and calls for its travellers to reorganize their actions, thoughts, feelings, and perceptions in ways that will make them different from most of the people around them. This is not because warriors are required to enter a monastery or live as recluses on mountaintops. On the contrary, they are highly skilled at living among the masses, but their ways of understanding the world and bases for decisions will guide warriors away from indulging in many of the feelings and behaviors of their neighbors and colleagues. This conjunction and separation from the ordinary world is exemplified in the selection criteria for some Gurdjieff groups and Feldenkrais Trainings. The ideal student is seen as someone who has already demonstrated success in the usual pursuits of society, or success in some field of endeavor, but who is still dissatisfied. Finding that the everyday measures of success lack something of importance, the warrior candidate seeks more.

There are many options available for the person looking for a path, and we are not interested here in judging the value of one type of path relative to another. There is one very salient factor, however, that we can use to decide if a path is right for you. The key factor seems to lie in choosing a path based on whom you are in essence, and in finding a way that is suitable for your interest, enjoyment, and development. Carlos Castaneda received sage advice from his mentor in *The Teachings of Don Juan* when he was given the question:

> Does this path have a heart? If it does, the path is good; if it doesn't it is of no use. Both paths lead nowhere; but one has a heart, the other doesn't. One makes for a joyful journey; as long as you follow it, you are one with it. The other will make you curse your life. One makes you strong; the other weakens you.[1]

The message here is that there are many paths, and the end of each path is the same. Ultimately, we are all going to die no matter what path is elected. Meanwhile the question is, how do we choose to live our lives? Don Juan is saying that we are free to choose, and he gives the above guidelines for assessing if we have made the right choice. If we discover that our chosen path does not have heart, we are free to choose again. If you have chosen a path with heart, you have fulfilled one essential requirement of warriorship, for don Juan says, "It is the consistent choice of the path with heart which makes a warrior different from the average man."[2]

Within the warrior's way there are many options, many paths. Some stem from an oriental view of the world, some from an occidental view. Some paths evolve from ancient teachings, some from modern ones. The source of the path and the particular trappings and structure that define it do not determine its value for you. If the path has heart for you, if it fits with your essence, if following it strengthens you and makes a joyful journey—even while requiring discipline—then you have already begun to live like a warrior.

Although warriors choose their paths with heart consistently, they are not given to proselytizing or advertising. Those who are teachers will make the path available to those seeking their help, but the casual observer may not even be aware that the warrior has chosen a specific path. This is because most people are caught up in habitual patterns and have forgotten that such choices are possible. Besides, the path may not be obvious, and the warrior, eschewing the limelight, continues on her path without need of popular recognition.

In *Way of the Peaceful Warrior,* Socrates explains, "Much of the warrior's path is subtle, invisible to the uninitiated."[3] So, much of what the warrior does will not be noticed by people who do not know about choosing paths with heart.

The Warrior's Path

Choosing a path with heart marks the one who chooses as different from the mass of ordinary people. To select a path with heart, one must already possess a certain level of awareness, a level that indicates dissatisfaction with the consensus trance and informs the person that choices are available. Just how different the person seeking the warrior's path will become will be the subject of the rest of this chapter.

Engaging the Mystery

Castaneda writes of the warrior's path, ". . . it is the opposite of the life situation of modern man. . . . Modern man has left the realm of the unknown and the mysterious, and has settled down in the realm of the functional. He has turned his back to the world of the foreboding and has welcomed the world of boredom."[4] Here is the next juncture in the new warrior's split from everyday living. While others around her seek what is functional in living according to the program they have received from society, the warrior seeks the unknown. She is interested in finding new territory, making new discoveries, blazing new trails, and plunging new depths. All this can be done as the warrior takes care of business from day to day, if she is willing to find the unknown in the day-to-day realm and willing to disrupt her routines to pursue opportunities as they arise.

In *The Eagle's Gift,* Castaneda reports how Florinda, one of don Juan's fellow warriors, explained the nature of mystery to him. She described what was called simply "the rule," the precepts of which are:

1. "Everything that surrounds us is an unfathomable mystery."
2. "We must try to unravel these mysteries, but without ever hoping to accomplish this."
3. "A warrior . . . takes his rightful place among mysteries and regards himself as one."[5]

In travelling the path with heart a warrior must remain fluid, and the warrior's fluidity is greatly aided by engaging the world as a mystery, as Florinda describes. Should the warrior become solid in her perceptions, actions, or thinking, she will operate solely from habit and will become stuck at that point. She will think that she has found the "right" answer to each question or that anything outside what she already knows is nonsense. This is the end of the path with heart. The person who succumbs to the idea that she has found all that is worthwhile may continue to walk her path, but that path will no longer have heart. It will be reduced to mere exercise or ritual, and the path's effectiveness at bringing a more expanded and joyful life will never improve.

Feldenkrais cautioned his students against such solidity. He warned that once you believe you have discovered the correct way to do something, your learning is finished. Believing that you have found the correct way, you will not seek further improvement. Said in a different way, Feldenkrais is alluding to the idea that once the mystery has evaporated, there is nothing more to draw the interest of the explorer. The warrior, in keeping the sense of mystery alive, never shuts the door to the possibility of learning more. The mystery, the adventure of the unknown, is the fuel that propels the warrior along her path and energizes her quest for personal power and knowledge.

Related to the warrior's way of interacting with the world and oneself as mysteries is the ability to engage magic. As we will find in the chapter on magic, we are not referring to prestidigitation or the occult. Magic has to do with enhanced awareness and the ability to shift perceptions in ways that allow non-ordinary things to occur. Castaneda wrote about ways of *stopping the world,* which have to do with allowing perception and action to expand in ways that would ordinarily be impossible. Don Juan taught Carlos to stop describing the world through continuous internal dialogue that fixed reality in customary patterns of possibility. Only then could many of the non-ordinary experiences occur.

Trungpa relates magic to enhanced sense perception, which opens the perceiver to possibilities of deeper perception. Access to those possibilities was achieved by the Shambhala warrior through meditation practice, a most effective way of "stopping the world" and getting beyond internal dialogue, judgment, and personal history. Magic, in this sense, can only be practiced when the world is viewed as a fluid mystery rather than solid fact.

War

Using the term "warrior" to describe someone choosing the path with heart confuses some people who are unfamiliar with the warrior mythology. They use the term to describe heroic soldiers or fictional heroes like Conan or Rambo. In the context of the warrior literature described in this book, warriors seldom have anything to do with war. Although warriors can be called upon to be soldiers, they are actually seekers of peace. Though warriors aspire to fearlessness, they shun bravado and taking unnecessary risks. So, if the term warrior does not relate to war, why use it?

The application of the term "warrior" comes from the type of discipline and focusing used by ancient warriors to prepare for battle. To maximize the chances of surviving, the warrior led a disciplined life that gave self-mastery and a way of being in the world that was beyond what ordinary people could manage. It is this tradition of discipline, preparation, and self-mastery that forms the core of the modern warrior myth. The formula for success in battle has been adapted for success in life.

Life itself is much like battle. Survival is not guaranteed. There are no survivors on this earth—none of us are getting out of this alive! Even the master warrior of old eventually succumbed, either dying in battle or life. The object was how one fought and how one lived. If you were good enough you would survive this battle, realizing you had another yet to face. Battle is actually a metaphor for life.

The warrior, in her approach to life, is not oriented to conflict, but to struggle. There are many struggles to be engaged in, as we will see later when we investigate how warriors seek impeccability. Most of these struggles are internal—struggles against self-importance, against binding habits, against the state of sleep that most of us take for waking—and the battleground is our own psyche. The new warrior must be prepared for these struggles, and the preparation must be as meticulous as if going to war. Survival is at stake continuously, if not in terms of vital signs, certainly in terms of quality of life.

Don Juan taught that each act a warrior engaged in could be viewed as a battle, and that each act, given our mortal state, could be our last battle on earth. When the warrior treats each act as if it is her last, she will maximize the quality of that act. You can imagine the caliber of life that would emerge from a position like that. There would be no more fruitless worrying, no more cringing from an uncertain future, no more procrastination. As don Juan said, "Acts have power, especially when the person acting knows that those acts are his last battle. There is a strange consuming happiness in acting with the full knowledge that whatever one is doing may very well be one's last act on earth. I recommend that you reconsider your life and bring your acts into that light."[6]

There is one other thing that should be said about the warrior's relationship to war. There are times when warriors are called upon to be soldiers and to fight; so the objections to war are not based on moral grounds, but emerge from the process of living like warriors. War is often based on self-importance and identification, and to an impeccable warrior fighting over these issues is contrary to the struggle to rid herself of them. Nevertheless, warriors often have defended their families, villages, or countries when attacked. The warrior's objective in times of conflict is simply to end the conflict. Dennis Leri, a long-time kung fu student, says, "The Chinese have a term, *Chih Ke,* which means if you are forced into a conflict, to fight is wrong and to not fight is wrong, i.e., one must not do anything more or less than is necessary to resolve the hostilities."[7] If telling a joke will end the conflict, the warrior tells a joke. If drawing a sword is necessary, the warrior uses the sword with just enough power and precision to stop the fray.

The word "war" is a part of the word "warrior," but the warrior does not seek war and does not seek conflict. Her goal is the end of these things and her conduct is determined with that goal in mind. The warrior walks her path with heart, preparing herself as if each act is her last battle, knowing that her focus is life itself, not war.

Death

Associated with the warrior's relationship to war is her relationship with death. We know the warrior views each act as her last battle, which means that she expects her death at any time. Rather than becoming immobilized by fear of death, the warrior turns it to her advantage. She learns to use death as her advisor. Castaneda recounted don Juan's belief that death is an entity that stays just behind one's left shoulder. Under the right conditions you can even catch a glimpse of it. Since death is always there, the warrior turns to death for advice. If unclear about how to act, the warrior asks her death. Death will remind the warrior that this act may be her last battle on earth and that she should act accordingly. In so acting the warrior could recall Trungpa's words, "You can never avoid death. . . . But if you have lived with a sense of reality and with gratitude toward life, then you leave the dignity of your life behind you."[8] Death will advise the warrior to act with impeccability, to do her best, to follow her path.

Being keenly aware of her death does not make the warrior morbid, obsessed, or depressed. Instead of becoming preoccupied with death, the warrior regards it with detachment and uses it to her advantage. Death puts the warrior's life and actions into the perspective of a mortal being. The warrior, being aware of her mortality, knows she can waste neither time nor energy. "An immortal being," according to Castaneda, "has all the time in the world for doubts and bewilderment and fears."[9] The warrior, taking advice from her death, knows that this is not true for her. Since she may have no time left, she must live impeccably in each moment. Knowledge of her death also helps the warrior to feel courageous and free. Trungpa defined cowardice as "trying to live our lives as if death were unknown."[10] In contrast, having death as a nearby presence gives the warrior courage to face anything. As Castaneda wrote, "Don Juan said that the worst that could happen to us is that we have to die, and since that is already our unalterable fate, we are free; those who have lost everything no longer have anything to fear."[11]

Taking a path with heart leads the warrior to relate to death in ways very different from how people commonly relate to it. The average person, fearing death, tries to put it out of her mind and acts as if her death is irrelevant. Time and energy are spent in all sorts of frivolous ways that do not relate to living with the sense of direction that comes from being on a path with heart. Being intimate with death, in a way that is neither morbid nor grim, adds vigor and cognizance to the warrior's life. Trungpa sums up this point by writing, "We don't know how long we will live, so while we have our life, why not make use of it. Before we even make use of it, why don't we appreciate it . . . existence is wonderful and precious."[12]

It is important to understand that the warrior, while having a straightforward relationship with death, is primarily oriented to life. The warrior is not drawn to death and does not abandon herself to it. The only preparation for death a warrior makes is to tighten and tune her life, to live it fully. So strong is the warrior's affirmation of life, explained don Juan, that "his death must struggle to take him. A warrior does not give himself to it."[13] Trungpa taught that a warrior neither seeks nor flees from death. Instead, she lives her life in keeping with her discipline and her commitment to warriorship, travelling the path with heart as long as she lives. "Even for the warrior, there is no victory over death," wrote Millman, "there is only the realization of who we all really are."[14]

Life

The warrior's relationship with death does indeed determine her relationship with life. The certain knowledge of death's inevitability is ample motivation for the warrior to seek to maximize who and what she is. This involves the development of one's capacities. Feldenkrais taught that most people usually operate at a level of five to ten percent of their capacity, except in activities in which they have a high degree of specialization, or in unusual circumstances. He suggested that if you improved yourself only two percent above this baseline, you would be considered a genius. Warriors are interested in this improvement and even more. As a warrior increases her personal power and has more of it to apply to her actions, she can function at a higher level. When this higher level of functioning is used to promote better warriorship, even more personal power is gained and the warrior can continue becoming more and more capable and effective.

Part of developing one's capacities is the process of overcoming limitations that are acquired during the formation of personality. As will be discussed in Chapter Five, personality represents a self-concept and package of actions, thoughts, and feelings that are, for the most part, acquired from other people through education or imitation. Many limitations we experience have nothing to do with our inherent abilities; rather, they are the products of how other people imagined us to be, or how they projected their own limitations. But walking a path with heart requires integrity, which leads to knowing yourself for what you really are. With this knowledge, limitations acquired from other people that do not truly apply to us can be set aside.

Warriors are surprising in terms of how capable they are in so many aspects of life. It is not enough to be a "jack of all trades, master of none." Warriors may become masters of many things, or at least capable of functioning in many capacities. They learn a wide variety of skills, acquire knowledge in many areas, and enhance the development of all parts of themselves. This enables a warrior to relate to her life altogether, without having to work around gaps in her personal development that lead to blind spots and weakness. Trungpa wrote in *Shambhala* of how the journey of warriorship "brings a feeling of being a truly human being. Physically, psychologically, domestically, spiritually, we feel that we can live our lives in the fullest way."[15]

One other aspect of how warriors relate to their lives is that life is lived as a challenge. Don Juan believed this and explained, "His [the warrior's] life is an endless challenge, and challenges cannot possibly be good or bad. Challenges are simply challenges."[16] Living like this means the warrior is not overwhelmed by sudden changes in circumstance. The warrior is used to meeting challenges, and since challenges are neutral, she is not devastated when one comes along that other people would label "bad." Because of this outlook warriors are not subject to violent swings of mood in response to changing external conditions. The warrior simply accepts challenge as a part of life. Trungpa agrees, writing, "There are, of course, constant challenges, but the sense of challenge is quite different from the setting-sun feeling that you are condemned to your world and your problems."[17]

To Be or Not To Be

Castaneda was taught "We choose to be warriors or to be ordinary men. A second choice does not exist. Not on this earth."[18] DeRopp agreed, stating that one chooses to be a warrior or a slave. Choosing a path with heart represents the decision to be a warrior, to embark on a lifelong quest to unfold one's being and to acquire knowledge. Taking this fork in the road leads to a life that is both a part of the ordinary world and apart from it. Because the warrior usually remains in the world and deals with it successfully, she is a part of the ordinary world. However, the warrior sets herself apart from the boundaries of that world and conducts herself according to the strategy she has set for walking her path.

Society, culture, and government are constantly involved in the setting of boundaries and limits. They take as their primary task the creation of order, and go about doing so by drawing lines and putting things in their assigned places. This kind of imposed order is anathema to the warrior. In seeking the unknown the warrior must transcend imposed boundaries. To adopt the determined order of society is to close out everything that is not already included in that order. Society's determination to maintain the status quo, if successful, would forever banish the unknown. It would exile the mysterious, and in such a climate we would come to know more and more about less and less.

Great discoveries—the ones that change the course of history, that lead to paradigm shifts—are not made by thinking within the limits prescribed by convention. No, these discoveries are made by those who, no matter how capable they are of following rules, sometimes step over the lines and engage the unknown. It is only there, in the mystery, that new discoveries and prototypes can be found.

Without the warrior spirit there would be nothing new—no new thoughts, no new theories, no new methods. All things would remain within their places, and boundaries would become more and more rigid. The only conceivable end for a civilization, a society, or a world like this is extinction. Warriors won't stand for it.

Rejecting stagnation and extinction, warriors place themselves outside the boundaries and order imposed in the ordinary world. They are committed to crossing lines and even sometimes erasing them, preferring to move in open space in search of the mysterious. New knowledge is not to be found in the partitioned cubbyholes of the status quo that government and tradition enforce. Therefore, in seeking knowledge the warrior adopts anarchy.

The anarchy of the warrior is not the anarchy of the delinquent, but of one who lives in congruence with her highest truth and innermost predilection. Her path with heart will lead the warrior into unknown territory, which means she must have the freedom to cross boundaries, which in turn means that she cannot be contained by the established system. The warrior is aware, however, that living outside traditionally imposed law and order requires the highest levels of honesty and integrity. This is because the warrior lives by a more significant order—that imposed by her path with heart. This order does not dictate fixed boundaries and partitions, but provides powerful guidance for living like a warrior in a fluid, organic manner. The order governing the warrior's life does not furnish guide-lines, but guide-processes. It is an order that steers the warrior in and out of both the ordinary realm and the mysterious, an order that prescribes growth rather than stagnation.

Nelson Zink understood the warrior's relationship to society. At one point in *The Structure of Delight* Noom says, "To institutions and religions and governments, an unlimited mind is a dangerous thing. A lot of folks have much invested in their limits."[19] Zink also understood the difference between the delinquent's anarchy and that of the warrior. He illustrated it with the following story:

> Noom stormed into the house one afternoon after a confrontation with Boondoggle. When the screen door slammed, Derry looked up from her needlepoint to see what the ruckus was.
> "That mule is just plain rebellious."
> "Oh, no, child. Boondoggle is a different kind of mule entirely."
> Noom found a slice of pie in the pie safe and brought it to the table to eat. He began to eat and the old woman folded up her needlework, putting it away in her work basket. "You see there are rebellin' types of mules and then there are revoltin' kinds of mules."
> "Well, he's ornery."

"Oh, no. That's where you're wrong 'bout Boondoggle. Now most of your mules are rebellin' types, but that's where ol' Boondoggle is different. Rebellin' is not doin' something that somebody wants you to do. That's when you're just an ornery cuss, not doin' what somebody wants just to spite 'em."

"Well, that's what he's doing," Noom complained between bites of pie.

"No, I think you've got it wrong. You see, when you don't do what somebody wants you to do, that's rebellin'. But if you do what you want to do then that's revoltin', and Boondoggle is a revoltin' kind of mule. He don't care so much what you think is right as he does about what he thinks is right. Rebellin' is when you want to hurt somebody and revoltin' is when you want to help yourself. So in a funny way rebellin' is when you say 'no' and revoltin' is when you say 'yes.' Rebellin' is when you fail at revoltin'. Mules are famous critters for rebellin', but Boondoggle is famous because he's a choice-makin' mule."

"Well, I don't like him very much."

"Oh, child. He always gets the upper hand because you're always rebellin' with him. Start revoltin' just like him and you'll get along fine."

Long after Noom left Missouri he remembered the choice-makin' mule with considerable fondness. For it was Boondoggle who taught him the subtle but life-shaping difference between rebellion and revolution. Taught him that rebellion kept one bound in conflict and revolution freed one of it.[20]

The warrior, in living by the order of her path with heart, must expect to come into conflict with society's imposed order from time to time, and she must choose between rebellion and revolution. The choice is clear because the warrior is dedicated to change, to expansion. Growth, expansion, and change all disrupt the status quo because they lead to something new and different, and the warrior should not be surprised to find resistance from those devoted to current beliefs and practices. Like Boondoggle, warriors know the difference between the rebel's anarchy and the revolutionary's anarchy. The warrior anticipates the resistance of others, adapts her strategy to deal with it, and then follows her calling. After all, she has already passed the point of deciding to be, or not to be, a warrior.

Living Strategically

Taking the warrior's path with heart requires strategic living. This means that the warrior is committed to her path and adjusts her activities and her life to further that commitment. Robert deRopp, describing Gurdjieff himself, wrote, "It is the chief characteristic of an impeccable warrior that he lives strategically, never does things by halves, prepares meticulously in advance, and enters the battle knowing what risks he is taking."[21] A warrior's strategy is designed to bring her commitment into action, develop her being, and enhance her knowledge. Living strategically requires the warrior to eliminate impulsive, whimsical actions and cease being a slave to her likes and dislikes. Actions and decisions are to be based on the warrior's strategy and have a well-considered quality to them, even when undertaken with lightning speed. To abandon one's strategy is to abandon the path itself.

If we examine it, we will find that living strategically involves, among other things, setting a direction and following it. The warrior can steer herself in the desired direction even through delays, distractions, and accidents which would knock the ordinary person off course. The warrior stays with her plan unless, through due consideration, she concludes that a change in course better serves her strategy.

Another apparent deviation from her course, which is not a deviation from strategy at all, is that warriors can grasp what Castaneda called the "cubic centimeter of chance." According to don Juan:

> All of us, whether or not we are warriors, have a cubic centimeter of chance that pops out in front of our eyes from time to time. The difference between an average man and a warrior is that the warrior is aware of this, and one of his tasks is to be alert, deliberately waiting, so that when his cubic centimeter of chance pops out he has the necessary speed, the prowess to pick it up.... A warrior ... is always alert and tight and has the spring, the gumption to grab it.[22]

Being prepared to grasp those cubic centimeters of chance is part of strategic living. In their training warriors deliberately tune their systems to recognize the chance and to move swiftly enough to seize it.

In living strategically warriors follow an unbending purpose and develop an unbending intent. They are able to bring their will to bear on circumstances so that intent can become manifestation. Castaneda explains how warriors acquire unbending intent in *The Fire from Within*. He says that it "begins with a single act that has to be deliberate, precise, and sustained. If that act is repeated long enough, one acquires a sense of unbending intent, which can be applied to anything else. If that is accomplished the road is clear. One thing will lead to another until the warrior realizes his full potential."[23] Acting with unbending intent focuses the warrior's power through the lens of her strategy and makes her effective in transforming decision into action.

Living strategically and being guided by unbending purpose calls for preparation, which the warrior gets constantly through her training and exercises for developing impeccability. The warrior's strategy leads her to be in control. She is in control of herself because she has synchronized her body, mind, and spirit, and has learned how to apply her power and abilities toward actualizing her intentions. Although warriors can apply their personal power in ways that affect the outcome of events, the control they have is really self-control. Vincente, one of don Juan's party of warriors, explained to Castaneda," . . . the challenge of a warrior is to arrive at a very subtle balance of positive and negative forces. This challenge does not mean that a warrior should strive to have everything under control, but that a warrior should strive to meet any conceivable situation, the expected and the unexpected, with equal efficiency."[24] Efficiency and control both advance the warrior's strategy.

Responsibility

"A warrior takes responsibility for his acts; for the most trivial of his acts,"[25] according to Castaneda. Responsibility does not refer to taking blame or accepting fault; rather, it means that the warrior acknowledges that she makes her own choices, imposes her own rules, and pursues her intentional aims. In acknowledging her responsibility, the warrior completely removes herself from the role of victim. People who attempt to victimize or manipulate her are dealt with as petty tyrants, as described in Chapter Five, and used by the warrior to further the task of eliminating self-importance. When presented with unforeseen circumstances, the warrior accepts them as her latest challenges. Therefore, the warrior cannot be a victim of either people or events.

There is an absorbing exercise that illustrates the potency acquired when full responsibility is taken. Take a finite period, say a week or a month, and adopt the extreme position that you are responsible for everything in your experience. Take responsibility for what you do, feel, think, and say. Take responsibility for all that you perceive and experience. Take responsibility for everything that happens to you, for all aspects of your life, for everything you witness. This will show you what it is like to abandon the position of victim and withdraw from people and events the power to exploit or harm you.

At this point you may argue that the sky *really* is blue and that you had nothing to do with it. However, the point of the exercise is to take responsibility for your *perceptions,* not for reality, whatever that may be. At present you only know reality through your perceptions, and perception is an active event in your nervous system. The quality and content of perceptions are variable and relate directly to such things as your ability to focus attention, your attitudes, and your beliefs about what is possible. Regardless of the ultimate status of reality, taking responsiblility for your perceptions will enhance your ability to enlarge and diversify your possibilities of perceiving.

A friend once told me that she could not do this exercise because if she were responsible for her experiences, she would be responsible if she got sick. She believed that making herself sick would be stupid and, therefore, if she got sick she would be an idiot. This is adding insult to insight. It is not part of the exercise, but we can gain insight about how we judge ourselves and we can take responsibility and control over that. The point is that taking responsibility withdraws the seat of power for your life from the external world and gives it back to you.

Since the warrior is responsible for her experiences and decisions, she acts without reservation. This is not impulsiveness, though. Actually, the warrior considers things thoroughly. Her decisions are the result of calculations as complete as she can make them. She appraises all factors fully because she wants to leave nothing to chance. The warrior lives on the basis of personal power, and by applying her power the role of chance is reduced. Thus, the warrior deliberates, even when it must be done with blinding speed, to avoid being surprised. She considers deliberately because once she begins to act there will be no time for further pondering.

The hallmark of the warrior's actions is commitment. Like a singer reaching for a high note, the warrior must commit her resources to the act or it will fail. A rock climber in the middle of a difficult move cannot be considering other moves or thinking about other things if she is to stay on the rock. Deliberations and calculations belong to the stage of preparation. Since the warrior takes responsibility for her acts, she cannot afford doubts, second guesses, or vacillations. When it is time for action, only awareness, responsibility, and personal power count.

Castaneda wrote a great deal about how the internal dialogue that people maintain keeps them from acts of power, and Feldenkrais said, "Internal dialogue, thinking or whatever you want to call it is a holding back from action. It is the rehearsal of an act or action. When there is complete commitment to an action, no matter how small and subtle or how large and violent, if it is complete and there is no holding back, then there will be no internal dialogue."[26] Acting with this kind of commitment is a true expression of the warrior's spirit.

The warrior's responsibility continues after an act has been completed, as the warrior takes responsibility for the outcome and for the consequences of her decisions, no matter how long they last. She learns from her experience, still without thinking in terms of fault or blame. She assembles what she has learned without arrogance, self-righteousness, or self-pity. Nor does the warrior take time for complaints, recriminations, or regrets. These are the prerogatives of immortal beings, but the warrior's death tells her she has no time for them. For the time has come to turn her attention to the next challenge.

Nowness

Another way in which the warrior's life changes once she has taken her path with heart is that the preoccupations of normal living are replaced with a sense of living fully in the moment. Trungpa says, "The challenge of warriorship is to live fully in the world as it is and to find within this world, with all its paradoxes, the essence of nowness."[27] In so doing one comes to experience the sacredness present in the moment. Trungpa equates living in the past or future with corruption—corruption of the present—and that is the only time when enlightened living can occur. He advocates awareness of one's personal situation, especially domestic and family life, as a marvelous ground for focusing on nowness. Despite your grand vision for society or your quest for illumination, when a child is hungry or happy, that event is happening now and needs your attention in the present. "Vision and practicality can be joined in nowness,"[28] Trungpa says. Without a strong sense of the present moment even the grandest vision is weak. If you have insufficient power to take care of your personal domestic situation, and if you cannot apply your vision in your life right now, there is little chance you can effect some positive change in the larger social, political, or economic spheres. In fact you may, without intending to do so, make things worse. Start with where you are, apply your grand vision to your own life; then you are ready to change the world.

Living in the future is usually a form of imagination, and in later chapters we will find that uncontrolled imagination is a way to lose personal power. Not that a vision for the future is bad, but failure to institute that vision in the actions and situations of the present leads to ineffective living, chronic disappointment, and even a cheapening of the vision itself.

Living in the past is likewise detrimental. DeRopp, writing about a major challenge in Ouspensky's life, described how Ouspensky carried a strong sense of nostalgia for pre-Bolshevik Russia. From his observations deRopp concluded, "Nostalgia is fatal to the spirit of the warrior, whose task it is to live in the here and now, not hankering after the past or fussing about the future."[29]

Travelling the path with heart promotes living in the present, which is the only time the warrior's power can be fully applied. A sense of nowness leads the warrior to organize her personal life so that it fits with what she believes and is consistent with the requirements of her path. From this base the warrior can reach out to other arenas and there will be no conflict between what she practices and what she says. Each moment contains the entire universe, and the warrior's sense of nowness enables her to flow from one moment to another, focusing her attention and power in the present, and harvesting the magic the moment has to offer. For, as Dan Millman discovered, "There are no ordinary moments."[30]

Walking the path with heart changes the lives of those who walk it and gives them certain perspectives on and approaches to life, some of which have been examined in this chapter. Furthermore, the path with heart changes the attributes of the people and develops them into warriors. Some of the important qualities that unfold are presented in the next chapter.

Chapter Three

Power and Impeccability

THERE ARE MANY ways to think about power, and in this chapter we will try to differentiate them and relate them to warriorship. Power can refer to the ability to do something, often something paranormal, such as the ability to predict the future, know things at a distance, read minds, or manifest objects or occurrences. Power also can allude to the unseen forces behind the ordinarily observable world. This is a religious or mystical view. Most of this chapter, however, will consider the notion of personal power, since this is the primary fuel that propels the warrior on his quest.

Special Powers

Many people who develop an interest in warriorship are attracted by the lure of powers, special powers that will give them the ability to do things that most people cannot. Many of these could be called psychic powers, but in the mythology of warriorship this term is not usually used. The ability to wield these powers comes into play in the realm of the unknown, where reality is altered from the consensual definition so that special powers are possible. The way in which this could happen is examined in the chapter on the unknown.

Though paranormal powers occur, they are not an important part of the warrior's path, and people who enter the way primarily to acquire special powers have lost their direction almost from the beginning. As Socrates says in *Way of the Peaceful Warrior,* "Special powers do in fact exist. But for the warrior, such things are completely beside the point."[1] They are beside the point because they are not what the warrior seeks. Special powers are seductive and lead one to think that he has arrived at some special state of grace or superior level of development. It is all too easy for many people to become completely sidetracked from the warrior's quest and to become satisfied with the powers they have learned to use.

This is similar to what happens in meditation when powers and visions occur. They can make the meditator lose track of why the path of meditation was begun. Lawrence LeShan, in a very useful little book aptly called *How to Meditate,*[2] gives an example of a monk whose prayers were visited by visions of the Virgin Mary. He became very excited by this, convinced that he had entered some special state of holy grace. Still, the abbot knew that this vision was illusion and told the monk to spit in her face the next time she appeared. Even such an appealing illusion entails all the pitfalls of the more ordinary illusions that confine us. The warrior and the meditator are after bigger game, whether it be called knowledge or enlightenment, and getting attached to special powers is a sure way to get sidetracked. In defining magic in the context of the Shambhala warrior tradition, Trungpa says, "By magic we do not mean unnatural power over the phenomenal world, but rather the discovery of innate or primordial wisdom in the world as it is."[3] It can be very interesting, even useful, when special powers or paranormal events happen, but the warrior must use them in context without letting special powers disorient him from the path.

Unseen Power

In the literature on warriorship, reference is made sometimes to unseen power or powers that lie behind the ordinary world. Since the mythological warrior literature is predominantly secular rather than religious, unseen power is not named or deified. It is usually just called power. Don Juan said that power determines the fate of men and other beings, and he frequently guided Castaneda on journeys where he encountered strange beings and forces—what he called the inexplicable and unbending forces that make up the world. There were times when Carlos thought he must surely be in the presence of God, but Don Juan always explained that this was not so.

J. G. Bennett, in explaining Gurdjieff's cosmology, defined several levels of powers that are in charge of the earth and ever expanding ranges of the universe. He says there is a hierarchy operating that culminates in the "absolute," and that the powers humans can sense are on a much lower level. In many conventional religious teachings there are also powers that operate at an intermediate level. Angels would be an example of a power from the non-ordinary realm, but the angels are not God.

Personal Power

The writings on warriors deal with the notion of personal power throughout, but they seldom attempt to define personal power directly. Usually they imply the definition by describing how a warrior's life is different when he has personal power and what he can accomplish by becoming more powerful. Castaneda probably makes the closest attempt at a definition when he says, "Don Juan had set me up to live exclusively by means of personal power, which I understood to be a state of being, a relationship between the subject and the universe, a relationship that cannot be disrupted without resulting in the subject's death."[4] Despite the seriousness of Castaneda's words, this definition still does not explain much. Nevertheless, we can use his idea as the basis from which to clarify the meaning of power.

We could think of personal power as a form of energy bequeathed by the relationship with the universe, as Castaneda alludes. Perhaps this energy is the life force itself. An elementary scientific definition of energy is the ability to do work, and personal power may be the ability to live (that is, to do work) in a certain way that results in unfolding one's potential and expanding one's knowledge of the universe by forays into the unknown. This will lead to further development of one's relationship with the universe, since the warrior will know the universe in a broader and deeper sense. This deepening relationship bestows even more personal power on the warrior.

All living beings have personal power. A being has a distinct identity and is identified by some kind of border, usually a membrane such as skin, that separates it from its surroundings. Having such a membrane requires the being to be in relationship to its surrounding universe. Before or after incarnation there is no such relationship. Depending on your belief system, there is either no existence or there is a unification with the universe. In either case there is no relationship because a relationship requires at least two parties. Besides, the notion of personal power is moot if there is no person.

Living as a person means there is some kind of division between yourself and the surroundings, and your continued existence necessitates a relationship with that universe. The self cannot survive without it. The skin separates "me" from "not me," but the "me" is dependent on the "not me." The membrane separating the two must be semi-permeable because an exchange of energy with the environment is necessary.

Living beings convert matter into energy through the alchemy of breath, digestion, and metabolism. Just as importantly, they must give off substances that would be toxic or disruptive to the life functions of the organism. To the organism these are waste products. If you watch horses eating in their fields you will see them taking in large quantities of grass, processing it, and converting parts of the grass into energy and then giving off the remainder as manure. To the horse the manure is waste. To the beetles in the field and to the grass plants, though, the manure is food. The grass then uses the manure in its own metabolism to grow new leaves and the cycle continues. It's a beautiful example of natural recycling. Horses and grass live in a balanced relationship, each feeding the other. The relationship will remain balanced as long as the "waste" is recycled. If it is not recyclable, like many waste products of humans, the balance is upset and environmental degradation occurs. The point is that living beings get energy from the universe around them by living in relationship with the universe. The basis of the relationship is the exchange of energy.

Castaneda realized that this relationship is necessary for life and that the quality of the relationship varies. By improving it a person can exchange more energy and use the energy more efficiently. This is the substance of personal power.

Being alive means we have personal power by the nature of our energy exchange with the world around us. You might say that we have a basic ration of personal power to stay alive and to function. Yet, the warrior does not settle for the basic ration of power that produces a basic level of existence. He seeks more power so he can live at more effective and efficient levels. Therefore, he must expand and enhance his relationship with the universe. The point of acquiring more power is to improve one's ability *to do.* Gurdjieff was concerned with the ability *to do,* and it is worth reviewing his ideas at this point.

The Ability *To Do*

Gurdjieff taught that people are subject to scores of natural laws, and by developing one's being and knowledge, freedom from some of them could be attained. The person could then come under the influence of higher laws. Since most people have relatively little development, largely due to insufficient personal power, they are subject to the law of accident. This means that what happens to most people, and their reactions to what happens, are not under their control.

Though this is true, most people believe they are in control of their lives and that they have the power to enact their decisions and desires. Gurdjieff maintained that this is an illusion and that most people cannot follow any course of action for any reasonable length of time. Usually the flow of important events of an ordinary person's life has to do with the accidents that come his way. If a person is moving along one line of action and his line crosses another line of action, an accident occurs. If the person has sufficient personal power he can maintain his direction, but most of the time ordinary people are swept away along the new direction, whether they intended to go that way or not.

But warriors live strategically, which means they can formulate a plan and follow it. Once they have this capacity they can become free of the law of accident, because plan is opposed to accident. Only when one can follow his own line of direction and not get sidetracked by intersecting lines does he become free of the law of accident and begin to live under the law of cause and effect.

In ordinary life planned actions are very rare. Sometimes one's plan may coincide with accidental happenings. Then people quickly take credit for having accomplished something on their own power, and their illusory beliefs in their capability *to do* are reinforced despite many more examples to the contrary. Only with a sufficient amount of personal power can one *do* what one wants. Don Juan pointed out that attaining this ability is a mark of warriorship when he told Castaneda, "A warrior actually affected the outcome of events by the force of his awareness and his unbending intent."[5]

Another way of talking about the warrior's ability *to do* is to say that he is fully functional. Feldenkrais taught that to function one must formulate a clear intention. Then he must have the power to actualize that intention. If either of these parts of the function is deficient, dysfunction will occur. Following this line of thought, Feldenkrais went on to define a neurotic person as someone who begins to do one thing and ends up doing something else. The action taken might vary a small amount from what was intended, or it might be something completely different. The neurotic becomes filled with anxiety because experience soon teaches him that he has a very low probability of succeeding in his actions. The neurotic does not function very well and is limited in the types of behaviors in which he can engage. The more neurotic a person is, the farther from warriorship he is. The warrior has the clarity to formulate intentions and the power to actualize those intentions.

So personal power brings with it the ability *to do,* which is a primary characteristic distinguishing a warrior from an ordinary person. Both begin with a certain power ration. But what happens to it? The answer is that we spend it, and everyone chooses—either through awareness or default—to spend it in certain ways. Warrior and ordinary person must spend power to stay alive. Beyond this the question is, how do you want to live? Feldenkrais said that most people aspire to a happy-go-lucky state of mediocrity. With this choice power is spent on survival and the rest goes to what we will call power sinks and power leaks.

The warrior's choice of how to spend his power springs from his recognition that something other than mediocrity exists. He believes that life is more than trying to get by, hoping to avoid trouble. There is a recognition of the *more*. To live effectively means to be able *to do*, and the warrior knows this takes power. Consequently, the warrior strives to use his ration of personal power wisely and productively. This means he tightens his life and cleans up his act so that he wastes as little power as possible. In the warriorship literature this is called *impeccability*. By reclaiming power from power sinks and by plugging power leaks, the warrior sets out to expand his relationship with the universe and claim even more power. He uses this power *to do* even more effectively and to continue his quest for an ever expanding relationship with the universe.

To expand one's relationship with the universe it is necessary to contact parts of the universe outside the confines of what one already knows. In other words, one must hunt power in the unknown. This is the core of the warrior's life—all other things a warrior does, from practicing his discipline to coming to terms with fear, are designed to facilitate and empower this quest.

Impeccability

The importance of efficient, effective use of personal power can hardly be exaggerated because personal power is the key to the warrior's existence. Robert deRopp asserted that he had only two possessions—his personal power and the time he has between now and his death. It is personal power that enables one to use the time to attain freedom. It is personal power that enables the warrior to travel the path with heart. It is personal power that enables the warrior to develop his being and improve his knowledge. It is entirely too precious to waste, and because personal power is so necessary, the warrior seeks to gain more of it.

According to don Juan, "Everything in a warrior's world depends on personal power and personal power depends on impeccability."[6] This sounds clear enough but, as often happens in the warriorship writings, the explanation of the main concepts is vague and the meanings must be gleaned from many dialogues, stories, and examples.

As with the definition of personal power, the definition of impeccability must be summarized by inference.

One way of defining impeccability is to say it is the ability to do one's best always. It is the conscious application of one's resources to the matter at hand. To do this it is necessary to be fully awake, free of mechanical responses, and aware of what you are doing and how you are using your personal power. Acts done with impeccability are acts of intent, not acts based on accident, self-importance, identification, imagination, or any of the other power leaks we will soon explore.

This capacity to act in ways that free power for the warrior's use seems to be the core of impeccability. Impeccability means the leaks are plugged and power is available to the warrior. This available power is also a definition of impeccability. As don Juan tells us, "The only thing that counts is impeccability, that is, freed energy."[7] To be impeccable, then, is to act with freed energy, with personal power that has been snatched away from the multitude of power sinks and leaks that plague us.

Often impeccability is mistaken by the uninitiated for morality. Castaneda often thought that he was being given moral guidelines for behavior when what don Juan was doing was outlining methods of promoting impeccability. This is illustrated in *The Fire from Within*, as don Juan tells Castaneda of the nature of sexual energy. "I have always told you that sexual energy is something of ultimate importance and that it has to be controlled and used with great care," he said. "But you have always resented what I said, because you thought I was speaking of control in terms of morality; I always meant it in terms of saving and rechanneling energy."[8] Warriors are not guided by religious or moral tradition, no matter how humane or wise these may be. Such guidelines are for others who, if they actually live by the restrictions, will manage to live a relatively happy and decent life. For warriors, though, such external codes do not apply. The warrior must develop internal guides that come from the struggle for impeccability. Let us now look more closely at how power is lost and how warriors can reclaim it and become impeccable.

Chapter Four

Power Sinks

A POWER SINK IS much like a pond or lake in the desert with no outlet to the sea. Power collects there, but being unable to flow, it just evaporates. It is useful only in its own little area. A power sink is a mechanism that binds power to it and makes power unavailable for other pursuits. Actually, there is really only one power sink—habits. We will also talk about beliefs, a special sub-set of habits, and follow that by examining a particular type of belief called the truth.

Habits

As don Juan said in *The Fire from Within*, "Warriors, since they have to enter into the unknown, have to save their energy. But where are they going to get energy, if all of it is taken? They'll get it . . . from eradicating unnecessary habits."[1]

Most people have a staggering profusion of habits—habits of behaving, habits of perceiving, habits of feeling, habits of thinking. By their very nature habits exist beneath the level of awareness and can influence how a person functions in ways scarcely imagined.

As an example, take a moment right now and clasp your hands with your fingers interlaced. It feels familiar, doesn't it? This is something you've done hundreds of times without even thinking about it (never mind that it takes several dozen muscles to perform this small act). Notice how the fingers are positioned. Which thumb is on top? Which small finger is on the bottom? Now, shift the interlacing of the fingers one notch, so that the other thumb is on top and the other little finger on the bottom, with all the other fingers shifted accordingly. For most of you this will feel weird, almost like these are not your hands doing this. Just this little change has taken you into the realm of the nonhabitual and you can tell it feels very unfamiliar.

Try holding hands with someone with whom you usually hold hands, and you will find that as a couple you have an habitual way of doing it. If you deliberately hold his or her hand in the nonhabitual way you will get a very interesting reaction. When you notice your reactions to doing these small things nonhabitually you get a feel for the amount of energy tied up in the habits. If a relatively meaningless habit like finger interlacing has such energy stored, think about the amount of power required to maintain an habitual way of walking, speaking, working, or viewing the world.

It will be interesting for you to examine small habits systematically for the next couple of days, just to sense the amount of energy they consume. Try putting your pants on with the nonhabitual leg first, or try putting the other shoe on first. Try brushing your teeth, shaving, or putting on make-up with your non-dominant hand. The difficulty you experience and your emotional reaction will show you how much power is required to maintain these habits. It is like grabbing a rope trailing a coasting locomotive and using your energy to try to stop it from rolling. It appears that the locomotive is expending no energy, yet there is a tremendous amount of energy present, in the form of momentum. If you want to find out how much energy there is, just try to stop the locomotive with your own strength. The amount you work shows you how much energy was bound up in the locomotive's motion.

So far we have only discussed small habits of little importance. Can you imagine how much power is allotted to habits that are important? In the next chapter we will discuss the process of identification in which you invest something of yourself in some object, pattern, idea, or habit. When you invest a habit with the notion "This is me," a tremendous amount of power is consumed in maintaining that habit. To maintain your habitual appearance, habitual life style, habitual relationships, habitual identifying characteristics, you will invest vast quantities of your personal power. You can test this idea by acting nonhabitually in one of these important arenas in which you define your personality and observing the amount of energy that you generate in your reaction and the amount of resistance you mobilize as your automatic patterns struggle for reinstatement.

For warriors, habits are dangerous in other ways than binding up their personal power. Remember, habits affect not only behavior, but perception, emotions, and thoughts. Attitudes become habitual, emotional responses become associated with certain situations and become automated, and you can only perceive the world in certain habitual fashions. By your habits you restrict the range of possibilities of experience, and all the other possibilities—the rich range of actions and responses—are not available and sometimes cannot even be imagined. This poses a great restriction in a person's versatility of functioning, and restricting choice is inconsistent with the warrior's way.

Habits of thought and belief determine, in large part, our self-concept, and that concept will determine the way we perceive our possibilities. If some skill or experience lies outside our habitual self-concept, there is little chance that we will even try to engage it. This artificially limits what we can attain and what resources we can use for growth.

The deleterious effects of habits are described throughout the warriorship literature. Castaneda talks about the amount of energy that is consumed in maintaining habits. Trungpa speaks of how habits promote traits that are damaging for warriors, particularly the trait of arrogance. He writes, "Arrogance comes from lack of gentleness . . . lack of gentleness comes from relying on habitual patterns of behavior."[2] No one is more arrogant than someone who is so caught up in habits that she cannot understand how another person can interpret things in a different way, or can desire to do something differently. Such people have little tolerance for differences among others, and their imprisonment in their own habits forms the basis for all sorts of bigotry. Because habits are so strong and responses so auto-matic, the bigot never sees the value in anything outside her restrict-ed circle, and all sense of gentleness and compassion is lost in the arrogant attempts to establish these habits as the proper world order. This illustrates a process the warrior must strive to overcome. As Trungpa goes on to say, "By clinging to habitual behavior, we are cutting ourselves off from the warrior's world. . . . We use our habit-ual patterns to seal ourselves off and to build ourselves up."[3]

Trungpa describes a principle of Shambhala warriorship that he calls *drala.* This will be discussed in the chapter on magic, but now we will note that Trungpa taught that warriors can tap into a source of magic in the world that can connect one's own intrinsic wisdom with a sense of greater wisdom or vision that exists beyond the warrior. Habits can interfere with this ability, and Trungpa writes, "Once we overcome habitual patterns, the vividness of the drala principle will descend, and we will begin to be individual masters of our world."[4]

Socrates taught Dan Millman the effects of habits on warriorship. Socrates characterized the differences between himself and Dan one day when he said, "Your feelings and reactions, Dan, are automatic and predictable; mine are not. I create my life spontaneously; yours is determined by your past."[5] In another part of *Way of the Peaceful Warrior,* Millman caught Socrates enjoying a cigarette and became upset at finding his teacher, who had tutored him in many practices of purification, engaging in such a disgusting act. Socrates told Dan that there were rare times when he enjoyed tobacco and that "Smoking is not disgusting; the habit is . . . I have mastered all compulsions, all behavior. I have no habits; my actions are conscious, intentional, and complete."[6] It takes an advanced warrior to live in such a way. Since our abilities of self-deception are so great we must be careful not to excuse harmful behavior by rationalizing that it is conscious when, in fact, it is impulsive or automatic.

The negative effects of habits were examined at length by Gurdji-eff, who taught that ordinary people are very much like machines. The processes of education and acculturation induce a profound, trance-like state more similar to sleep than wakefulness. Because it is so familiar, people believe themselves to be awake in this state; but compared to the experience of genuine self-consciousness, they are indeed in a trance. In this trance most of their thoughts, actions, perceptions, and feelings are automated, which means that they are utilized and invoked habitually by circumstances and rarely by conscious choice. Charles Tart in *Waking Up* calls such a state of consciousness "consensus trance." It is the usual state of consciousness for almost everyone, and the common consensus is that everyone is awake. But this is illusion. Compared to what it would be like to by truly awake, ordinary consciousness is much more like sleep. In Gurdjieff's teachings and on the warrior's path the only way to freedom from consensus trance is to wake up.

Feldenkrais described many ways in which habits restrict. He asserted that most people are so programmed by their society that they develop very little after reaching adulthood, which is around the age of sexual maturity. After that time growth takes place primarily in terms of developing specializations in vocation or avocation. Overall, most people use about five to ten percent of their capabilities, except in certain areas of vocational or avocational specialization. The other ninety to ninety-five percent becomes dormant, and since we rely on acquired habits, it never occurs to us that we can tap that great reservoir of unclaimed capacity.

Feldenkrais pointed out that all too often people learn how to do something in only one way. The ensuing habitual performance does not imply mastery, no matter how good a person gets by doing it that way. If you only know one way to do something, there is no choice in how you will do it—there is only compulsion. It is only when you can do something three or more ways that you begin to use your human intelligence, to act by choice, to obtain freedom from habit, and to attain mastery. Most people, though, become satisfied when they can produce results in a given way. Warriors cannot accept that, for as Feldenkrais explained, once you become satisfied with your results, your learning is finished. You will no longer feel motivated to improve. Warriors know that improvement is infinite; that perfection can only be approached, never attained. Warriors, in this sense, are never satisfied but seek to act impeccably, all the while knowing that they have not attained their maximum capacity.

Release from Habits

"You're going to have to change habits of acting, of thinking, of dreaming, and of seeing the world,"[7] said Socrates to Dan Millman. No less is in store for us who seek to follow the warrior's way. We have already considered how unnecessary habits bind personal power, so let us explore ways of releasing ourselves from habits that do not serve the warrior's quest.

The first tool the warrior employs in this endeavor, and in most of the pursuit for impeccability, is awareness. Habits by their very nature operate beneath the level of awareness and occur automatically. To change these patterns we must bring them under conscious control, which means that we must become aware of how and when we do them. Without awareness, we will continue to use habits in an automatic fashion and not even realize that we are doing things in the way we do them. Habits put us to sleep, induct us into consensus trance, and divert our power into the maintenance of the habits. It is necessary to awaken before we can grow and proceed on the path—and awareness is requisite to awakening.

Jean Houston tells a story about some wise men who approached the Buddha and asked, "Sir, are you a god?" Buddha replied, "No, I am not a god." Then they asked, "Are you a man?" The Buddha replied, "No, I am not a man." So the wise men asked, "Then what are you?" The Buddha said, "I am awake!"[8] Awakening involves making one's actions conscious and intentional as opposed to automatic and habitual.

In his work Gurdjieff recommends self-observation again and again as the principal pathway to awareness. It is necessary to learn exactly what you are doing and how you are doing it. Through the process of self-observation you can get an idea of how often you are not aware of what you are doing and how much of the time you spend operating with habitual patterns. This knowledge gives you the motivation to change, because those who would be warriors will find the results of their observations unsatisfactory.

Besides observing yourself as you act, sense, think, and feel in your usual ways, you can gain awareness of your habitual process and begin to bring your patterns under conscious control by deliberately engaging nonhabitual patterns. Castaneda was taught by don Juan to disrupt routines as part of his training in impeccability. If you try some of the practices mentioned earlier in this chapter about altering your habits, you probably will find it difficult to disrupt some of your small routines, such as the way you dress and groom yourself. Nevertheless, you will become much more aware of how you usually do routine actions. In the search for awareness and impeccability a warrior will question the value of all routines and will examine them thoroughly. She will keep those that are necessary and productive and will eliminate all others. Even so, the routines that are kept are no longer as they were before. Now they are under conscious control and done by choice. This leads to the warrior being awake for more of her day, and she will gain an impressive degree of flexibility in how she acts and reacts to the world and events in her life. In any situation in which old habits used to pop up she will have access to a menu of actions, including the old way if she finds it useful.

Engaging in nonhabitual patterns produces greater awareness of how you have done things habitually, and it also begins a process of releasing you from the habits. To do something in a nonhabitual way you must first become aware of how and under what conditions you act habitually and then you must develop options. You then experiment with these options, finding which ones are feasible and which ones are not, refining the feasible options so that they become more effective, and replacing old patterns when new ones prove more effective. Even when you decide to return to your usual way of acting, you will find that it has been enhanced by the process of exploration and because you have made a conscious rather than automatic choice to do it that way. You are now functioning with intent, which is a very powerful way of living.

The Feldenkrais Method is a potent way to overcome habits. In many countries of the world, classes in Awareness Through Movement® are offered. Feldenkrais developed this method so that he and his practitioners could reach many people at once. Lessons often begin with the students lying on the floor and directing their attention to the way in which they organize their bodies while remaining passive. Each person will find several idiosyncrasies, such as the head or pelvis being slightly rotated, the small of the back being arched away from the floor in a certain way, or one side of the body lying in a different way than the other.

Although many beginning students do not think this information is very important, it is actually a rich source of knowledge. What they are sensing is their underlying, habitual organization that permeates every voluntary action they undertake and colors how they interact with the world. Sometimes in workshops I have people experience what it is like to gently roll the heads of several others who are lying on their backs, with instructions to remain completely passive unless they perceive what is being done is not good for them. If these instructions are followed, the people lying on the floor disengage from voluntary levels of activity and organization. Yet every head rolls in a unique way, which indicates that there is another level of organization that is active. This is the habitual level, which influences all that is done, regardless of whether we do it consciously or automatically. This is the level the students are asked to sense while examining themselves as they lie on the floor at the beginning of a Feldenkrais lesson. It is at this level that the Method seeks to produce change.

After the body scan is done, a movement is suggested, and since the lesson is just beginning, the students do it in their habitual way. It is fascinating that they have habitual ways of moving, even if they have never done the specific movement. The movement is usually done slowly, well within the students' comfort zones, and the emphasis is on observing how they are trying to do it. Becoming goal-oriented, competitive, or trying to please the teacher reinforces the tendency to act habitually and make learning more difficult.

Having done the movement for the expressed purpose of increasing awareness of how one engages in the movement, the class is then guided through a series of variations on the general theme. Many of these variations are nonhabitual and disrupt the ways in which the participants use their involuntary level of organization to accomplish intentional action. This produces awareness of parts of the body that may have been sensed only dimly in the past, highlights the limitations of habitual patterns, and offers alternatives that might be more efficient. Eventually the beginning movement is done again, but this time students find that they can do it with much less effort, and with greater comfort, range, and accuracy. Lying on the floor and scanning themselves again, the students will find that they have a greater sense of awareness of themselves and that the way they organize themselves on a passive level has changed. Perhaps there is more symmetry, or greater relaxation, or something that was painful is now comfortable. Whatever the sensations, something has changed in the habitual level of organization. Often there are accompanying changes in mood or attitude, and at times sensory changes such as improved visual acuity or brighter perception of colors.

Whether you go to a Feldenkrais class or not, the model is very useful for releasing habits on the way to developing impeccability. First it is necessary to acquire awareness of how you do what you do. Then, armed with this self-knowledge, consciously introduce variations, bringing the action to a higher, nonhabitual level of control. In the process, do the action so you can stop at any point along the way and either resume, reverse, or discontinue the motion. By this point you are no longer acting on automatic and, at least in the immediate situation, the habit has been broken. Generalizing this learning to other situations requires using vivid, controlled, imaginal rehearsal of yourself functioning non-habitually in other situations or actually going into those other situations and practicing the nonhabitual processes. Simply making a resolution to be different will not work. You need an active, fully developed alternative to the habit that will have at least as much survival value as your habit did, to gain your freedom. You also need a strategy for developing options and control.

Feldenkrais drew on Gurdjieff's "stop" technique in developing his ideas about how to learn efficient movement. Practicing this technique will help you discover if you are acting in control or acting automatically throughout your day. Periodically tell yourself to "stop!" If you can stop what you are doing immediately, you are under control; if not, you are acting automatically and are not in conscious control of yourself. Another similar application is to stop momentarily when you make the decision to do something, as there is always a slight time lag between decision and action. Use this interval to decide whether to proceed or not.

If you are stuck in finding new options to explore, you can try putting the habitual manner "out of bounds" and engage the situation anyway. At areas where rock climbers practice they soon become familiar with the holds necessary to complete any particular practice climb. To increase the challenge and make the familiar unfamiliar, they put the key hold of the crux move out of bounds and then climb the pitch. You can do this not only with actions, but with habitual points of view, emotional responses, and problem-solving strategies. You also can imitate how other people respond or act, putting your own way on hold. This is an incredibly rich source of variations.

You can use these techniques for movements, thoughts, or feelings, and when you begin to use them you will no doubt be amazed at how much of the time you act automatically. When you have discovered what you do and how you do it, you can begin to disrupt your routines and habits to free the power bound up in this power sink.

Conscious Control

People often assume that the opposite of habitual action is to think about every aspect of what they are doing as they are doing it. This would be incredibly tedious and ineffective. Your habits would probably serve you better. In this book, conscious control has a different meaning.

Feldenkrais asserted that the only conscious part of an action is the decision to make it. Therefore, it is important to get clear on what we mean by conscious, or higher level, control. We are not talking about guiding each phase of an action with the intellect, or in Fourth Way terms, the thinking center. This is not possible, as any golfer or skiier well knows. When thinking starts, action stops, even if only momentarily. If you observe a person who is trying to think her way through an action, the motion is jerky and lacks fluidity. This is because she is momentarily engaged in evaluation and re-deciding. If she takes a long time with this, the action has a noticeable pause. If she is quick about it, it will just be jerky and clumsy. In effect, thinking the action through breaks it up from one continuous action into multiple actions that may not blend smoothly. In a sport like golf, requiring great precision, the gaps in blending produce inaccurate shots. In a fast sport like skiing such discontinuities can result in falling.

Conscious control, rather than thinking your way through the action, means that you become very good at decisions, the only part of the action that is conscious. Making decisions requires choices. It is necessary to cultivate a wealth of skillful options for any particular activity or class of activities. These become the menu from which you consciously choose. The choice is conscious, not because of thought processes, but because of awareness and freedom from automatic compulsions.

As a beginner in a given activity your task is to identify the requisite skills and learn to perform them. Often, the thinking center tries to dominate the process, resulting in many errors. That is why instructors begin teaching golf on the practice range, skiing on the bunny hill, and swimming in shallow water. You want to avoid disaster during the learning period and reduce anxiety.

While learning, it is often helpful to take a complex action and break it down into manageably sized chunks. Ideally, the chunk size is small enough that the novice can soon learn to accomplish it without having disrupting thoughts. These chunks can then be expanded or combined so they can be approached as a single action. In this way the learner can acquire a basic competence. It is only basic competence because the learner only has one way of accomplishing the act. Even though skillful, she has only one choice point—to do it or not. Mastery begins by learning other ways. So, when the beginning golfer can hit a straight shot, she is ready to move from the practice tee to the course, and the skiier moves to steeper or more complicated terrain.

Once this happens, the learner finds that the basic skill is not adequate for all the conditions encountered. So it is back to learning and practicing other options. The golfer learns to hit low shots that roll and high shots that land softly; she learns shots that curve to the left and shots that curve to the right. She must learn these skills so well that she can do them without interference from her intellect. Acquiring these options gives the student more and more choices and puts her on the road toward advanced performance.

We can now say that our golfer is playing under conscious control. In response to changing conditions she selects her clubs and shots from her repertoire, then commits herself to the action without thinking and changing decisions during the swing. If she must change her mind she has to do it at a time when the resulting pause will not produce problems.

At this point the golfer is fortunate. The game includes time for analysis and deliberation. The skier seldom has this time; nor does a basketball player, a jazz musician, or anyone else engaged in an activity of speed. In fast actions one makes conscious decisions in response to changing conditions almost instantly. To do this you must eliminate self-talk, or what Castaneda called internal dialogue. Subvocalizing imposes a speed limit on thinking that is tied to how fast the vocal muscles can move.

Feldenkrais illustrated this point by the following exercise: First, count from one to ten. Now count from one to ten twice that fast. Continue trying to go twice as fast and you will soon find you cannot increase your speed of counting beyond a certain point if you sound out the numerals. Furthermore, Feldenkrais pointed out that usually a person can count from one to ten much more quickly than from twenty-one to thirty. The number of digits is the same, but the words are longer and take longer to say. One way to get past this speed limit is to count visually without sub-vocalizing the numerals. Soon you can go from one to ten at an internal glance.

In NLP this is called streamlining the strategy. By streamlining your decision strategy regarding actions, and by stopping internal dialogue, you can make decisions so rapidly that breaks in the action interfere as little as possible. You decide and adjust decisions in response to conditions with a strategy that is so efficient and rapid that any breaks in the flow of action are so small they do not disrupt the action.

Instantaneous decisions are also made that adjust the accuracy of one's own motions. This is a feedback process in which actions are matched against the original decision and discrepancies corrected. There is a beautiful complexity involved in making the original decision. The specific form and parameters of the choice are actually fabricated in the moment of deciding. Because situations vary continuously, responses must also. Therefore, we are not talking about employing an inflexible diagram of an habituated action and comparing our performance in the moment to that. It is more complex and wonderful than what some theorists refer to as application of a specific "muscle memory." It is unlikely that muscles are capable of learning or remembering anything. Dr. Karl Pribram, director of the Stanford University Neuropsychology Laboratory, calls what you learn *the image of achievement,* and it is a function of the nervous system. When you learn an action well you learn more than the specific sequence of muscles tensing and joints moving. You learn the entire pattern. This allows you to write your name in any size letters without having to learn that specific size from scratch. Because of this you can learn to sing a song in the key of E, but you can sing it in A also, even though the muscle movements are quite different. Deciding to do an action generates this image, which is probably stored in the brain in a form more akin to a laser disc than a photograph, and the brain will mobilize whatever parts of the body it can access to accomplish the action. If the action produced varies too much from the *image of achievement,* the brain will adjust its use of the body accordingly. The senses feed back information about the accuracy of the action and the brain makes adjustments. People often experience a noticeable mismatch between action and image as a feeling in the body. This feeling tells them something is amiss, but the internal process can only be done quickly by minimizing or eliminating verbal thinking. By the time you pronounce the words it may be too late.

In effective action both processes are smoothly engaged. Choices of actions are made from an adequate variety of options, and specific forms and scope of action are generated in the image of achievement. During the action, whole new images may be chosen as needed, and the accuracy of performance is monitored and corrected continuously. During a ski run, for example, the skier makes hundreds of decisions. Some of these are larger decisions on the order of choosing where and when to turn, to accelerate, or to slow down. Others are micro-decisions about such things as shifting balance, changing head position, altering pressure on the soles of the feet, or breathing. The feedback mechanism and a streamlined decision process produce actions that are accurate and continuous. They are not automatic stimulus-response habits and they are not produced by internal dialogue. This is conscious control.

There are times when the actions proceed so smoothly, with conscious control operating so unobtrusively, that the action seems to flow of its own accord. Records are broken and sterling artistic performances accomplished when people are in this zone. It is a remarkable and awesome display of capability and intelligence. Dan Millman writes of several of his gymnastic experiences that occurred in this way and he calls it *meditating an action*. It is high-level, conscious control and represents freedom from automatic, habituated processes. Now we turn our attention to some habitual processes that do not necessarily involve overt action.

Beliefs

A type of habit that deserves special mention is beliefs. Nelson Zink says, "Belief is the fossilization of meaning, belief is meaning formalized."[9] Holding habitual beliefs binds energy in the same way other habits do, and the warrior wants to free that energy for use. To maintain a rigid belief structure requires an investment of energy in that structure every time the question of what one believes comes up. Beliefs become the filters through which we structure experiences. Therefore, they restrict what meanings can apply to experience and they restrict experience itself. Beliefs are very powerful—they have the power to organize one's entire world, to be the criteria for what is true, and to provide the boundaries between reality and fantasy. But they do not have their own power. The person has the power and invests it in the belief. The warrior must decide if this is a useful investment of personal power. As we will see later, one can lose even more power if she defends her beliefs against those who believe differently. Thus, beliefs can be both power sinks and power leaks.

Belief, meaning, experience, and perception are nested within each other. Experience is the subjective effect of perception. Experience is what we take to be reality because it lies just at the interface between the inner and the outer world. Warriors realize that it is subjective, though it seems external. This is because it is as close to the external world as we can come.

Usually we interpret experiences by assigning meaning. Often this is done simply by naming something. Once it is in the province of the

60

intellect, we change experience into meaning. Rather than relate to experience itself, we take the experience as a symbol of something else and we relate to the symbol. It takes great discipline to do otherwise, to have experience without attaching meaning and turning it into a symbol. Zink's old Hawkeen warrior explained this to his apprentice, Jay, by saying, "There are those who believe that it is impossible to see at all without seeing with meaning, but it is possible. The naming part of your brain is where a lot of meaning is created, so the path to seeing without meaning begins with the shutting down of the naming department. . . . The process of perception is ongoing and naming stops this procession. When meaning is specified the world is complete and stops, set in concrete. A name turns the infinite into the finite."[10]

So the fluidity of experience is changed by meaning into something solid. Then the solidity of meaning is fossilized into a belief. Then that belief becomes the lens through which we allow ourselves to experience. This is a formula for restriction and impoverishment of experience, a far cry from the fluid life of the warrior.

Nevertheless, doesn't the warrior believe in something? Doesn't the world have meaning? The answer is yes. The difference is that warriors are flexible in their beliefs rather than rigid. They adopt beliefs by choice and can become free of the ones programmed in by other people. Robert Dilts, writing in the NLP book *Beliefs,* points out, "Many of the beliefs we have acquired were installed by the time we were five years old by your parents, significant other people and possibly by the media."[11] Warriors know this and distinguish between programmed beliefs and reality. Besides, warriors know that beliefs solidify a person's reality in a specific way, and knowing that there are many realities possible, they want to have multiple beliefs.

This is best illustrated by Zink in describing the Hawkeen. Noom says, "The Hawkeen are masters of belief. They collect beliefs and trade them, sell them or give them away. They invent them and bargain for them or steal them. Hawkeen will believe anything you want them to. They will believe everything and its opposite also. They know that beliefs are what make your head work, that a belief is what it does. The Hawkeen have a belief that the more beliefs one has, the more choices one has."[12]

Rather than being stuck believing in only one way, and having to defend that way against conflicting beliefs, warriors adopt a strategy of choice. They choose a belief that works for the circumstances at hand. They do not need to argue against a belief and certainly would not argue based on the assumption that some other belief is not true. Warriors select beliefs based on what works for them in life and on their quests as warriors. "The secret of a warrior is that he believes without believing," says don Juan. "A warrior, whenever he has to involve himself with believing, does it as a choice, as an expression of his innermost predilection."[13]

Truth

That warriors do not choose beliefs based on truth and do not argue or defend beliefs on that basis opens the door to an important idea—truth is an internal event and does not exist externally. When you believe something is true, it means that you have given it that meaning based on something you experience in your nervous system. In NLP this is called your belief strategy, or truth strategy.

Try something right now. Think of something that you *know* is true. Take your time and then ask, "How do I know that's true?" If you answer, "I don't know how, I just know," or "I accept it on faith," then you have more work to do. Slow the process down and notice all the components—what you see, hear, and feel internally as you think of your truth. For some there will be representations of taste or smell also. These are the components of experience and they exist prior to the meaning you assign. Notice also the qualities of each internal sensory experience. Vision may be lighter or darker, more in focus or fuzzy, closer or farther away, for example. Hearing varies in many ways such as pitch, tone, and volume. When these variables coalesce into the right configuration, you will know to accept the experience or idea as truth.

Now do the same thing with something you *know* is not true. Find how your inner experience is different. For most people, the key seems to be a certain feeling that they have about the idea or experience. If that feeling is present, the idea is accepted; if absent, the idea is rejected.

This means that truth is an inner experience. Most people want to project this feeling of truth onto something in the outer world. It's not enough to feel good about your church, it becomes necessary to project it outward as the one true church. You externalize your politics and claim you know the only way the country should be run. If other people disagree with your truth it must mean there is something wrong with them. Otherwise your truth cannot be true. After all, truth is absolute, right? This is how wars get started. This is the foundation of missionary work. One person, one group, one institution, or one country tries to impose its truth on others, either through force or "education." Thus, the communists conquered other countries to give them the true social system. The Spanish Catholics burned the Mayan texts and scriptures in order to give them the true religion. The capitalists exert international monetary pressure to bring others into the fold of the correct economic system.

Warriors avoid this process of externalizing truth. They sort their experiences based on what works and realize that any sense of truth comes from their internal experience. This does not make it true in any absolute sense, and they are free to use the Hawkeen strategy of choosing other beliefs when the current set fails to serve them. The truth is not worth fighting about because it is an intensely personal experience and has no absolute meaning. Think about how much energy would be saved if everyone tolerated other versions of truth and was not threatened by diversity. Warriors understand how much power is bound up in habits, beliefs, and the truth, and they set out to free their personal power from these power sinks.

The methods for doing so are similar to those for disrupting other kinds of routines. First become aware of the beliefs you operate from and what it is that you accept as truth. Then, putting expectations aside, examine the current situation from at least three different belief positions. Play "what if" by adopting a minimum of two other beliefs about the current situation and play the scenario through, either hypothetically or actually, and assess the experience in terms of what worked best about each belief position. Avoid getting caught in the trap of deciding which one was true.

It is also very useful to adopt someone else's beliefs for a day. Sense, think, and feel from the position of a different truth or belief system. Make decisions based on the other system and notice the outcomes of your actions. You will learn a great deal about what works and will become much more flexible in generating choices.

Chapter Five

Self-Importance

PEOPLE LOSE MUCH of their personal power through a variety of common power leaks. The leakages are so severe that most people maintain only enough power to survive and continue their lives with little more development than they had when first attaining adulthood. Sometimes the power leakage is so great that survival itself is threatened by stress-related disorders and accidents that could be prevented. The warrior must understand what power leaks are, the forms they take, and how to plug them in order to develop impeccability. Without impeccability there is not enough power to engage in the warrior's quest to any meaningful degree. Part of the process is to disrupt routines and habits while pulling power out of power sinks. The other part is to plug power leaks so that power does not drain away uselessly.

"Self-importance is our greatest enemy," Castaneda declares. "Self-importance figures as the activity that consumes the greatest amount of energy . . . one of the first concerns of warriors is to free that energy in order to face the unknown with it."[1]

Untold amounts of power are drained away through this leak, so let us take a good look at how it happens. First, it is necessary to discuss the nature of the self. Castaneda is referring to self-concept or ego identity, a picture of oneself that is held to be the real thing. Yet it is no more real than a photograph compared to a living, vital subject.

Ouspensky offers a useful dichotomy that can help clarify this point. There is personality and there is essence. Personality is the self that is determined socially and culturally. Essence is the true nature of one's being and is largely inborn, although essence can be developed by working on one's being through deliberate means that include reducing the influence of personality. Personality derives from acquired characteristics such as opinions, views, and habitual responses—most of which really belong to people other than yourself—and forms an outer layer for one's essence. Because of this shield, impressions and influences that can help essence develop are unlikely to penetrate beyond the personality. Essence and personality do not have to be enemies, for both have useful and necessary functions, but it is a grave error to confuse them or to let personality become so highly defended that awareness of essence is diminished and its development and manifestation become stunted.

The key element in understanding this power leak is the process of defense. Essence needs no defense, since it is beyond threat. Other than the requirements for physical survival, warriors need take no actions to protect their essences, since essence exists in such an elemental form the only danger is the warrior's lack of awareness of himself. External threats simply do not apply.

The personality self, on the other hand, seems to require enormous amounts of defense, and ordinary people spend vast quantities of their personal power in constant self-protection. What happens is that the personality becomes identified as the self, but the personality is composed of acquired baggage that stems from external sources. As such its authenticity is invalid from the start. Without an authentic basis, the personality is subject to a wide range of threats. The person who holds his personality to be his true self must defend an illusion in a way that establishes it as real—an enormously difficult task that is imperiled by even slight changes in circumstance. Once the person has established the fragile condition of presenting the personality as the self, any change, including other people's thoughts, is menacing. Constant self-protection is needed to convince oneself that the personality is safe for the moment, and an elaborate array of defense mechanisms develops to provide that protection.

Self-importance is a good term to describe this process, since the personality self is presented to oneself and the world as the true self. This is an obviously exaggerated statement of importance. Once convinced that we, meaning our personalities, are indeed this important we will go to tremendous lengths to maintain or enhance our importance in our own eyes and in others' eyes as well. A cycle is established in which self-importance continues to grow out of self-importance, with more and more power being invested in maintaining one's image. Threats against one's status seem to multiply so we have to defend our self-concept on multiple fronts. The resemblance to national defense policies and politics is all too obvious.

In *The Power of Silence* Castaneda provides a succinct analysis of the ultimate nature of self-importance and the reason it is an unproductive leakage of power. To quote don Juan, "Sorcerers had unmasked self-importance and found that it is self-pity masquerading as something else. . . . Self-pity is the real enemy and the source of man's misery. Without a degree of pity for himself, man could not afford to be as self-important as he is."[2]

Attack Thoughts

A Course In Miracles develops the concept of attack thoughts very well. We will illustrate the defense of personality using the notion of attack thoughts, rather than engaging in a lengthy discussion of a variety of defense mechanisms from the field of psychology. Besides, such defense mechanisms are nicely explained in Chapter 13 of Tart's book, *Waking Up*. The central point of this concept is that any thought about attack is an attack thought. When I have a thought that is critical or hostile about someone, I am attacking them and words or acts may be produced by these thoughts. Also included is the idea that when I think I am being attacked or criticized, or when I think that someone is having hostile or disparaging thoughts about me, I again am engaging in attack thoughts. The presence of any attack thought means that I am engaged in an act of defending my personality or ego self and stems from a position of weakness. I can even have attack thoughts about myself and spend still more energy defending myself from my own thoughts. Whenever I am attacking someone else, I am making a preemptive or retaliatory strike that is designed to protect me. Whenever I have a defensive thought, I am worrying about an attack and will expend energy in self-protection.

Attack thoughts are immediate indicators that I am engaging in self-importance. I have inflated the value of my personality to the extent that I am convinced I should divert my personal power from my growth into means of defense. For the warrior this is a mistaken set of priorities and signals that he is in a state of fear. As will be elaborated in Chapter Nine, a state of fear can mean that the warrior is disoriented and has lost his state of fearlessness. But warriors can sometimes use the fear state productively by tapping its energy to propel themselves beyond it. As Trungpa says, "True fearlessness is not the reduction of fear, but going beyond fear."[3] Indulging in attack thoughts is going the other way. It is an attempt to reduce fear by defense and counter-attack that does nothing but effect a temporary feeling of security at best. In the long run what has been accomplished is to validate the personality's importance so that personal power must be deflected from other interests to preserve it. We then establish a pattern that any time a threat is perceived, we mobilize our defenses. This strategy will never help us come to terms with fear and move beyond it, and we will expend enormous amounts of our resources for self-defense based on self-importance.

Psychology

Let us take a slight digression at this point to explore how modern psychology might view the issue of self-importance. Traditionally, psychology deals with the concept of personality at great length, but only with the outgrowth of transpersonal psychology catalyzed by the works of thinkers such as Jung and Maslow has the field had much to say about essence. The more common view is that strong ego defenses are a sign of health. The more secure you are in your self-concept and the greater your self-esteem, the more stable you are deemed to be.

As a psychotherapist, most of my early career was spent trying to help people develop a strong self-concept that could withstand threats. This was often done by establishing a strong sense of self-worth based on accomplishments and feedback about one's abilities to cope with problems the world presented. Later, however, when I learned more about the warrior's way, I began to have doubts about the validity of psychotherapy. What if, for all these years, I had been helping people to build strong self-concepts and thereby diminished their chances to cultivate awareness of essence? Have I condemned them forever to living in the usual way with all the drains on personal power that self-importance entails?

What made the issue more confusing was that all the people I knew who were involved in the warrior's path in one form or another appeared to have very strong self-concepts. They seemed to like themselves and were not easily threatened or worried. Moreover, people with low self-esteem never could handle the ideas and practices required by the warrior's way.

In reconciling this apparent contradiction I found that a sufficiently high level of self-esteem is necessary to begin the warrior's way. At the same time, an awareness of the limitations and pitfalls of self-importance is also necessary. If someone's self-importance is too low they channel all efforts, other than physical survival, into attack thoughts in the forms of avoidance, worry, and responding to imaginary threats. Being preoccupied in this way, people with low self-esteem do not develop skill at dealing with problems and tasks of daily living, and the person with such low self-esteem becomes truly inept at getting by from day to day. Warriorship is extremely difficult to pursue from this position.

If, on the other hand, a stable level of self-esteem leads to effective skills in dealing with the demands of the ordinary world, much less worry is called for. By analogy, if you know you can swim, water is much less frightening than if you cannot. A certain level of ego strength, then, is necessary to undertake the warrior's path. You can traverse little of this path, though, without the recognition that self-importance will cause you to lose your way and your precious self-esteem will need to be transformed. Acquiring ordinary world competence and ego strength is a developmental stage that usually precedes the warrior's path, like taking a prerequisite course. In that sense, becoming more competent in one's local existence, and drawing a sense of strength from recognizing that competence, can be the first steps toward warriorship.

Warriors are not easily threatened, not because of strong ego defenses, but because they are in touch with their essences and define themselves in these terms instead of completely identifying with their personalities. The warrior's way itself leads to competence in everyday living as personality is fine-tuned to deal with local existence. Therefore, warriors know they can swim in life's mundane waters and they commit to developing their essences and becoming less identified with their personality selves. Herein lies a new strategy for psychotherapy—to diminish threat by helping a client become more skilled as a life swimmer and by helping to contact essence as a source of security.

Don Juan explained this fairly straightforwardly to Castaneda in defining the *tonal*. Besides being the domain of all that can be known and dealt with by thought, the tonal is part of the make-up of human beings. It is the part that deals with the known. Don Juan explained that a warrior has a *proper tonal* and "The goal of a warrior's training then is not to teach him to hex or charm, but to prepare his tonal not to crap out."[4] In other words, a proper ability to deal with life—our analogous good swimming ability—is necessary to be a warrior. Even with cultivation of the tonal, however, warriors must never forget the requirement for balance by developing the other side of themselves. Warriors must have personalities that operate effectively in the world, but that do not diminish awareness or growth of essence.

Dealing with Self-Importance

Getting rid of self-importance is a long-term task accomplished in approximations. There may be some situations in which you operate unencumbered by self-importance and you think you have made great progress indeed. Then, without realizing it at first, you find yourself immersed in self-importance in a different time or situation. This is not a sign of failure. It is critical information. You are being shown another area for improvement, another arena in which to pursue warriorship. Without awareness of the situations, internal and external, in which self-importance arises in you, you are helpless to struggle with it. And just when you think you have conquered it, there it is again, showing you that you have not reached the end of your path. Fortunately, along this path there are tools to use in lessening self-importance.

The first tool has already been introduced. It is awareness. Without self-awareness, you are crippled in the battle with self-importance. If you are unaware of what you are doing, you will not know that self-importance is influencing you, and all progress will stop. One of Feldenkrais' favorite sayings was, "If you know what you are doing, you can do what you want." If you recognize you are leaking power to self-importance, you can do something about it. Gurdjieff stressed that self-observation is a critical skill in the harmonious development of man. It is your way of getting the information you need to combat illusions about yourself. Awareness tells you what is happening *now*—you must be willing to observe what you are doing. You can deny awareness you acquire and throw away the basis of action and growth, simply because awareness teaches you something you did not want to know. To be effective, you must court awareness and both recognize and use the data it brings to you. In so doing you will be taking a necessary step toward becoming an impeccable warrior.

Another way to struggle with self-importance is to cultivate humbleness. Don Juan taught Castaneda about the warrior's humbleness, saying, "The humbleness of a warrior is not the humbleness of a beggar. The warrior lowers his head to no one, but at the same time, he doesn't permit anyone to lower his head to him."[5] This theme of equality runs throughout the teachings about the warrior's humbleness. There is no debasing oneself and there is no judgment about one's superiority or inferiority in comparison to anyone or anything. There is no proclaiming of oneself and there is no denying one's own dignity. Trungpa advises, " . . . be very simple and feel that you are not special, but ordinary, extra-ordinary. You sit simply, as a warrior, and out of that, a sense of individual dignity arises."[6] The dignity arises not out of self-importance, but out of the knowing that you are on equal ground with everything else, as you follow the warrior's way.

You can develop the theme of equality that leads to humbleness in everyday life. Remember don Juan's words, "There is no end to the mystery of being, whether being means being a pebble, or an ant, or oneself. That is the warrior's humbleness. One is equal to everything."[7] Let regard for your surroundings and fellow creatures stem from this sense of shared mystery and equality. Spend time talking to plants. Catch the spiders in your house and release them outside instead of killing them. Perform service for someone else with no anticipation of reward, or even without anyone knowing it was you who provided the service. Willingly do such things—actions that an "important" person, such as your ego-self, would not do—and you can develop humbleness. As don Juan said patiently, "To regard the lion and the water rats and our fellow men as equals is a magnificent act of the warrior's spirit. It takes power to do that."[8] That power will come from plugging the leak of self-importance.

In *The Fire from Within,* don Juan explained to Castaneda a powerful technique for combatting self-importance. This technique involves using what don Juan called a *petty tyrant.* A petty tyrant is someone who torments someone else. The tyrant might be a person who is merely annoying, or someone with the power of life and death over others. Petty tyrants can torment through annoyance, apprehension, brutality, violence, sadness, or rage. Through encounters with such people, warriors develop a sense of detachment, for, as don Juan says, "Nothing can temper the spirit of a warrior as much as the challenge of dealing with impossible people in positions of power."[9]

We all have our petty tyrants, those who consistently provoke and irritate us, those we fear because of their ability to take our freedom, money, or status. Perhaps it's a boss who torments us, or a noisy neighbor, or a government official, or a punk on the subway. Whoever the petty tyrant is, he or she is proficient at getting under our skin and threatening us in some way. The tyrant tries to lure us into emotional reactions, and because we react we are victims of the tyranny. Remember though, we intend to be warriors, not victims. How interesting it will be to identify people in your life who qualify as petty tyrants and to adopt a warrior's viewpoint toward them. In so doing you will find yourself using these people's behavior as opportunities to practice the craft of warriorship rather than as sources of insult and annoyance.

What removes us from the victim's role is the warrior's ability to withstand the antics of petty tyrants without taking offense, without feeling threatened, and most significantly, without getting lost in self-importance. Self-importance will make us cry out, "It's not fair! It's not fair!" or, "Why me?" or, "I don't deserve this!" Once the petty tyrant has threatened our precious self-importance, we are in danger of losing personal power and being reduced to victims.

Warriors use petty tyrants to assist their task of self-observation so they can become aware of when they are engaging in self-importance. When the petty tyrant attempts his tyranny, the warrior exercises control, discipline, and forbearance, and when the time is right, he acts. The warrior, being determined to eliminate self-importance, does not take himself so seriously that he succumbs to the tyrants' manipulations. In essence, the petty tyrants' acts say, "You are not important!" Having developed his humility, though, the warrior takes no offense. Don Juan instructed Castaneda on this point when he said, "A warrior could be injured but not offended. For a warrior there is nothing offensive about the acts of his fellow men as long as he himself is acting in the proper mood."[10] Taking no offense, the warrior is free to act impeccably with the petty tyrant. He will do so, not from the threatened position of victim, but from the position of personal power conferred by his lack of self-importance. By dealing with petty tyrants, the warrior develops awareness, learns perspective, and diverts the energy freed from self-importance into impeccable action.

But what is impeccable action? It is action that uses personal power in a parsimonious way without wasting it on power leaks and inefficiency. Impeccable action is doing your best without regard to outcome, without trying to fake triumph or defeat. Impeccable action is undertaken with the full knowledge of your mortality, and knowing that death is inevitable, you act as if each action is the last step you will take on your path with heart. Impeccable action can be done only by minimizing self-importance, and therefore, you increase your personal power by plugging that leak.

It should be clear by now that self-importance must go if you are to become impeccable. Be prepared for this to take a lifetime, but begin right away. If you can reduce the amount of time you indulge in self-importance from ten hours a day to five hours a day, you have stemmed your leak significantly and saved a lot of personal power.

Then you can work on closing the leak even more. In your struggle to eliminate self-importance you have awareness, humbleness, petty tyrants, and your desire available to help you.

Chapter Six

A Morass of Power Leaks

Identification

IN *WAKING UP*, Charles Tart describes an exercise he does in workshops that demonstrates how power is lost by identification. Tart places a paper bag on the floor and directs the workshop participants to put their attention on the bag and to think of it as somehow being "me!" In other words, he guides them to think of the bag as a part of their identities. After a minute or so of this Tart stamps on the bag, and the participants react immediately. More than a startle response, their reactions are emotional and fearful. I have done a similar procedure with psychotherapy clients and the results are fascinating. Just like Tart's people, my clients react with shock, often as if they had been struck physically. Nevertheless, they quickly understand how easy it is to give something of yourself to something that is not your self. As Tart says, "It is all too easy to give the sense of identity to anything, and thereby give away some of our personal power."[1] This exercise is a demonstration of how the process of identification works.

Identification, as interpreted by Gurdjieff, Ouspensky, and Tart, is a process of defining oneself in terms of external or internal factors that are not oneself. We can identify ourselves as a variety of roles—parent, child, teacher, athlete, artist, and so on indefinitely. We also identify ourselves as characteristics—shy, bold, curious, fearful, serious, for example. Furthermore, we identify ourselves as our thoughts, attitudes, and values, believing that these things really define who we are. Most people identify with their bodies, and most also identify with groups—Christians, Republicans, Caucasians, New Yorkers. Many people identify with material possessions, some will even identify with a paper bag! The list could go on endlessly, but in identification the common theme is that you define something that is not your essence as your self, whether these are elements of personality or external things.

Castaneda does not use the word identification, but he dealt with a very strong identification present in most of us. Don Juan instructed Carlos to eliminate his personal history, and I take this to mean that Carlos was to cease viewing his past as what makes him the way he is. If you identify with your personal history and derive your sense of self from it, it will bind you strongly to your past, and you will have difficulty shucking off the chains of your old ways and venturing into new possibilities. What an enchanting idea—that you could be free of your history so you can be, act, think, and sense in any way you want. It's only possible if you withdraw your identification from your personal history.

Identification, as Carlos found, will restrict your versatility in action, and this is one of several ways it drains power. Tart discusses this and other means by which power is lost. First, identification produces a static quality in which permanence is both assumed and desired. Thus, we cannot adapt easily to the changing flux that life presents, and a great deal of power is used in trying to minimize any changes that might threaten the stability of our identification or the way in which we define ourselves.

Second, the beliefs, roles, things, groups, and words with which we identify are generally selected for us by others. Significant people, wanting to mold us into the shape and image that they designed for us, promote identifications that may be indifferent or contrary to our essences. This can lead us to spend our lives and untold amounts of personal power trying to live up to an image that was never really ours and can never express who we really are.

Third, identification occurs automatically and not consciously. If a particular identity really does not fit the demands of a situation, you can end up performing much below your true level of competence or acting in ways that are inappropriate. Through identification, stimuli automatically evoke certain perceptions and responses. Then we admit only habitual perception to awareness and act only in automatic fashion. Habitual and automated responses, feelings, perceptions, and thoughts work against the development of consciousness, as explained earlier. Furthermore, Tart points out that the automatic nature of identification interferes with the development of awareness of your essence, which is your true identity. Without awareness of essence it is unlikely that you can cultivate it, and your personal power will go into fortifying your false personality.

Gurdjieff described another way in which identification operates strongly, and to understand it we must return to his way of describing the self. This fundamental concept has to do with what Gurdjieff and Ouspensky called "I." Most people use this pronoun with little or no appreciation of the enormous illusion inherent in the way they use it. People think that there is a central self that operates continuously and that this self does not change. Such is the case, though, only in certain highly developed beings. For ordinary people there are many fragments of personality, each taking its turn masquerading as "I." Each fragment emerges mechanically in response to some set of circumstances and takes its turn being in the forefront. Therefore, we can believe one thing one day and act in a completely incompatible way the next day and not even notice.

Tart called each of these "I's" identity states, but deRopp labelled them much more romantically, and maybe more accurately, by calling them his ship of fools. Each fool takes a turn steering the vessel, and after a while another fool seizes the helm and may take off in an entirely different direction. The fools may have different preferences, different attitudes, different ways of justifying their courses of action. To foster awareness of this ship of fools some Gurdjieff groups have students avoid the use of the pronoun "I" and simply say "this one." Instead of saying, "I am sleepy," they say, "This one is sleepy." Or, "This one feels afraid," while the same student later says, "This one thinks being afraid is stupid." Only after years of work does a true "I" emerge that can steer the ship with consistency while drawing on all the skills and knowledge at the disposal of the former identity fragments on the ship of fools.

This entire process of having fools steering the ship takes place because of identification. We identify with whichever fool is steering at the time and believe this particular identity state is our self. Yet as soon as circumstances change and elicit another identity state, we identify with that one. This inconsistency in direction absorbs a tremendous amount of power and costs us the opportunity to find our true selves.

Cease Identification

Identification is the enemy of strategy. The process of identification—through which one member of our ship of fools after another steers us in whatever direction that particular identity state desires—diverts personal power into continual changes in impulse and direction. It is impossible *to do* while identified. In this state, according to Bennett, "Our will is wholly taken up with the dominant impulse of the moment"[2] in the state of identification, and the warrior's way of living strategically becomes impossible.

To cease identification, live strategically, and plug this power leak, we must turn first to our primary tool in the struggle for impeccability—awareness. It is necessary to be aware of when we are identified before we can cease identification, both in the moment and in our overall way of living. If you employ self-observation you will find several signs that indicate you are identifying:

1. To be identified means to be unaware of yourself and to be lost in an object, action, or idea. Ouspensky describes the state of being identified in a way that is at once accurate and vague when he says, "It is a certain state in which you are in the power of things ... it means losing oneself."[3] This refers to a state of being that is the opposite of awareness, since identification and awareness are mutually exclusive. When you find that you have been unaware of yourself and lost in your surroundings, you can be assured that you were identified.

2. Another indication of identification is defensiveness. Socrates explained to Dan Millman that, "What we identify with we tend to defend."[4] Defensiveness indicates the presence of attack thoughts, which means that you are functioning from the point of view of personality, not essence. Personality identifies with some belief or situation, and when that belief or situation is challenged, personal power is expended in a defensive effort.

3. The presence of negative emotions, according to Ouspensky, always indicates identification. In fact, Ouspensky asserts that, "Identification kills all emotions, except negative emotions."[5] Your emotional state, then, can be a productive ground for self-observation and detecting the process of identification. (Later in this chapter we will discuss negative emotions more extensively.)

4. Behaving or feeling inappropriate for the situation you are in can be a sign of identification, since having slipped into a particular identity state, you may not be aware that circumstances have changed. This will result in acting or feeling in a way that does not fit what is happening around you.

5. Difficulty accepting or adapting to change is often a sign of identification. A desire for permanence, which acts as a shield against change, will provide you with a potent clue that you are identifying.

6. Trying to live up to an image of what you should be or how you should act that is imposed by external authority is also an indication of identification. Identifying means that you are living by external reference points and are neither guiding yourself nor relying on your own power.

7. Inability to continue with a course of action, or in other words, not living strategically, indicates that you are identified. Losing oneself to distractions, ending up somewhere other than where you started to go, and being late because of factors of lesser priority than your original decision all indicate lack of strategic living and, therefore, identification.

Awareness, using these kinds of indicators of identification, is an absolute necessity if one is to cease identifying. In the teachings of Gurdjieff, and in those methods derived from his teachings, there is another critical technique to be employed against identification. It is called *self-remembering;* but as Ouspensky says, "Self-remembering is not really connected with memory; it is simply an expression. It means self-awareness, or self-consciousness."[6] Being in a state of self-remembering is, in many ways, the opposite of being in a state of identification. When you remember yourself you are not lost in your surroundings, your activities, your thoughts, or your feelings. You are radically present to the fact of your existence on the level of essence, and your personal power is available to apply to whatever you choose at the moment.

Tart describes self-remembering as a process in which we pull together the usually dissociated parts of ourselves into a unified whole, or as he puts it, "we have to *re-member* ourselves."[7] In a later passage Tart provides more detail, saying, "Self-remembering involves, among other things, the creation of an aspect of consciousness that does not become identified with the particular contents of your consciousness at any given time, and which can keep track of the totality of you. It is a partial to full awakening from consensus trance."[8] To self-remember, then, you must learn to employ some part of your consciousness as a guardian of the rest of your consciousness to keep you from getting lost in identification. This designated part must operate in a way that is free from identification to be effective. This seems like a reasonably straightforward thing to do; I just assign some aspect of myself to remain awake and not get caught up in all the silliness in which I usually engage. Yet in practice this is incredibly difficult to do because the habit of identification is so strong and can be so subtle that it is difficult to detect. The Fourth Way schools have many exercises that help to develop the ability to self-remember. A few of them will be discussed here, but reading about these exercises from books closer to the source is recommended, and if possible, working with someone who has had extensive personal involvement in Fourth Way techniques.

Gurdjieff once assigned Bennett a brief exercise in which he was supposed to remember to say "I am" at a precise moment during every hour. Bennett, though an exceptionally talented and resourceful student, failed completely to accomplish this apparently simple task without special help from Gurdjieff. He would get so absorbed in whatever was going on that he would forget that he had set his intention to do the exercise. It is a good example of identification. If you try this exercise you will find out that self-remembering is anything but easy in the early stages.

Tart also recommends begining your day with a structured morning exercise he called *sensing, looking, and listening.* The morning exercise involves paying close attention to the sensations arising in a designated part of the body, such as the left foot, and then a sequential tuning in to sensations from other parts of the body. This might take anywhere from five to fifteen minutes, depending on your ability to control your attention. After this you go back to the original part of the body, say the left foot, and then without losing awareness of that part, you gradually expand your attention to include the left leg, right leg and foot, left arm and hand, and right arm and hand. When you have included all these parts in your attention, you expand your attention again to include active listening to whatever sounds you can hear, without losing your body awareness. Having done this, you expand your attention again by opening your eyes and becoming aware of what you can see around you, without losing awareness of the body sensations or the sounds. Feldenkrais called this kind of process *inclusive attention,* as distinct from processes such as concentration that excude stimuli. In Chapter Ten we will find this inclusive kind of attention again in the discussion of Yoga.

As part of the morning exercise, this version of sensing, looking, and listening is done only for a few minutes, but you can employ the technique at various times throughout the day, expanding your capabilities so that, as Tart says, you "become so proficient at it that you can remember yourself for the rest of your life."[9] There is a great deal more information about sensing, looking, and listening, and about self-remembering in Tart's book. You are encouraged to gather more information about this very important, complex technique than space permits us to discuss here.

Negative Emotions

Negative emotions are treated differently depending on which branch of the warrior's path you are travelling, but the common theme is that such emotions can be serious power leaks. Much of popular psychology over the past twenty or more years has touted the benefits of expressing one's feelings, of "getting it out." The warrior literature has a much different outlook on the results of negative emotions, and it is interesting that in providing such a convincing psychological interpretation of Gurdjieff's ideas, Tart completely neglected to deal with the issue of negative emotions, perhaps bypassing the conflict between warriorship and psychology.

In *The Fourth Way,* Ouspensky is very straightforward on the subject of negative emotions. He says, "We must try to stop the manifestation of unpleasant emotions … the first step is trying not to express these negative emotions; the second step is the study of negative emotions themselves … and trying to understand that they are quite useless … they only waste energy and create unpleasant illusions. Thirdly … we can get rid of negative emotions."[10] Ouspensky believed that negative emotions could only occur in the presence of identification, and that they are not natural to a fully functioning human. Emotions, as viewed in his system, are controlled by a specific center in the person, but the emotional center has nothing to do with negative emotions, such as those that are violent or depressing. Negative emotions are thought to be controlled by a different center, but it is an artificial center that we create by imitating other people. When one of Ouspensky's students questioned him on this point and worried that the system would deprive him of his emotional life, Ouspensky told the student that until negative emotions are eliminated, he would not have an emotional life. That is to say, the true emotional nature of people cannot be attained while so much power is diverted into artificial, negative emotions. Eliminating negative emotions is one necessary condition that allows you to use not only the emotional center, but the higher emotional center, which will remain dormant until you attain a sufficient level of development.

Dan Millman agrees that it is better for warriors to inhibit the expression of negative emotion, although he appears to waffle a bit on this point from one book to the other. In *The Warrior Athlete,* Millman details how the dramatization of negative emotion is often a habit pattern that can be overcome. He points out, as Ouspensky would have agreed, that negative emotions are usually reactions to negative thoughts, and the behavioral expression of the emotion is automated and unconscious. Since warriors constantly struggle to overcome mechanicalness they apply conscious control to this progression. Millman writes, "You don't have to bring a thought or its corresponding tension to life; you don't have to dramatize it. You may notice a fearful thought; you may feel afraid—but you don't have to act afraid."[11] If you consistently act in a nonhabitual way when you experience the emotional obstruction (tension that is translated as a negative emotion), it will lose its strength as you withdraw your personal power from it. "Then, over a period of time," says Millman, "as emotional obstructions are left undramatized, they'll grow weaker until finally they become obsolete."[12] This brings you closer to emotional maturity, where true emotion is experienced as pure energy flowing freely in the body.

Millman is less definite about expressing negative emotions in *Way of the Peaceful Warrior.* In one part of the book Millman recounts how one of Socrates' former pupils watched his restaurant burn to the ground. The man sank to his knees crying, soon rose to his feet with a scream of fury, and then the emotion had passed. When Dan questioned him about this he replied that his strategy with such feelings was to "Let it flow and let it go."[13] Here, although the emotions of rage and sadness were expressed, they were not indulged in, and this example does not represent an habitual pattern. Socrates, in training Dan, consistently described true emotion as the free flow of energy in the body. Habitual employment of negative emotion, with dramatization, in response to certain types of situations impedes this flow of emotional energy. In his training Dan learned to transform negative emotions into positive energy, such as transmuting anger to laughter through right thinking.

When negative emotions are experienced and expressed in their usual, habitual ways they constitute serious power leaks. In addition, negative emotions stunt your growth, preventing you from attaining emotional maturity. Maturing in this sense begins with inhibiting the expression of negative emotions, which, accompanied by self-observation, will teach you a great deal about yourself and your reactions to events. You will learn how negative emotions are usually automatic responses to negative thoughts you can't control, and it will become apparent that to plug this power leak you must develop a proper frame of mind. As Millman says, "Only the mind free of meanings and judgments and expectations can allow the free flow of emotional energies—free of reactions of fear, sorrow, and anger."[14]

Another view on this subject is offered in *A Course In Miracles.* All emotions stem from either love or fear, but fear itself is only a cry for love. Fear is the province of the ego, the false self constructed through conditioning and identification, and when you feel angry, guilty, frustrated, bored, depressed, rejected, etc., the underlying emotion is fear. Fear is the habitual reaction to the presence of attack thoughts, and the presence of attack thoughts means that you have made a mistake in perception. You have most likely engaged either in judgment or have projected your fear outward so that you see it reflected back on yourself. Thus, you have lost contact with the basis of your true self—your Christ nature, as *The Course* would call it—or with your basic goodness, as Trungpa would call it. The presence of negative emotions, then, means you have made a mistake in perceiving the situation and that you have forgotten your nature. All the personal power contained in the negative emotion is expended in a mistaken direction and is wasted.

Struggle with Negative Emotions

Negative emotions drain an enormous amount of power. Warriors are willing to engage in the struggle to move beyond such emotions—and struggle they must, since negative emotions are very closely tied to identification. In addition, modern society often glamorizes participation in and expression of negative emotions. Many would argue that the ability to discharge emotions through expression is healthy, and that to suppress or repress them eventually causes an eruption of even worse feelings. This is not a view found it the warriorship literature.

The Fourth Way schools teach that negative emotions stem from an artificial center and that such emotions as anger, hostility, resentment, depression, boredom and jealousy are not natural to the human condition. They are, nevertheless, very common. In fact, the artificial function of negative emotions has replaced in most people what the Fourth Way schools teach is the vigorous, natural flow of emotions.

Therefore, on the path to impeccability, warriors must learn to free themselves from the grasp of negative emotions.

We have said much about the primacy of awareness in any aspect of acquiring impeccability. In the struggle with negative emotions it is essential to cultivate awareness of when negative emotions are being felt and being expressed. At times these emotions thrust themselves into awareness simply by their own strength. At other times their presence seems to lurk under the surface of awareness, coloring perceptions and choices, undermining impeccability, and draining power without our being aware of what is happening. Tuning awareness to the status of our emotionality is therefore essential in the struggle with negative emotions.

Ouspensky asserts that one of the primary steps in freeing oneself from negative emotions is to cease expressing them. Millman agrees and offers the parallel of muscles, which will grow with use and atrophy with disuse. Likewise, negative emotions gain power with expression and weaken when unexpressed. Though expressing negative emotions seems to discharge energy, the pattern of reacting to life with these kinds of feelings is strengthened with each expression. Thus, Ouspensky's advice to cease expression, coupled with the application of awareness, is a sound initial strategy.

Combined with awareness and cessation of expression, it is necessary to develop what could be called right thinking. Socrates pointed out to Dan Millman how thoughts can produce negative emotions when he said,"You have an angry thought bubble up and you become angry. It is the same with all your emotions. They're your knee-jerk responses to thoughts you can't control."[15] In attesting to the positive power of right thinking Socrates later told Dan, "You will be free of the world's turbulence as soon as you calm your thoughts."[16] Ouspensky urged his students to think rightly, and in recognition of the amount of power consumed by negative emotions, told the students that thinking rightly for six months would affect negative emotions.

Right thinking is adopting the warrior's view of life and ways of thinking about the world. When attack thoughts are recognized and released, all the emotions that are variations of fear are also released. When the warrior adopts fearlessness as a way of being she finds her thoughts are no longer fearful reactions or descriptions of a world in which goodness is a scarce commodity. When her thoughts interfere less and less with perception, the warrior can detect the unconditioned nature of the world, and negative emotions have no place from which to spring forth into her life.

With the warrior's growing ability to cease expression of negative emotions and to engage in right thinking, the personal power that had been expended will be available for the true emotional life of a warrior, which is the natural way for all people before the artificial function of negative emotions displaces it. As Ouspensky says, "Now we have no emotional life, but only an imitation."[17] Millman writes, "True emotion ... is pure energy, flowing freely in the body ... true passion, like that of the infant, is focused, free, relaxed—full of feeling and unobstructed energy."[18] Such progress leads to activation of the true emotional center, as described in the Fourth Way teachings, and eventually to activation of the higher emotional center. In order for the warrior to reach this level of emotional impeccability she has available Ouspensky's "Four Practices":

1. Study of negative emotions (including awareness).
2. Struggle with identification.
3. Struggle with the expression of negative emotions.
4. Right thinking.

In Chapter Nine there are some additional techniques from Millman and from NLP for dealing with emotions. You are not striving to suppress emotions, and you are not trying to lie to yourself about what you feel. Accepting what you learn with your awareness prevents lying to yourself. What you are trying to do is to disconnect habitual negative emotional responses from stimuli. When you are no longer in the habit of *having* to feel a certain way at certain times, you can develop emotional choice. When negative emotions abate you find new options for feeling, and this emotional freedom can lead to emotional maturity. The emotional energy can flow unobstructed through your system, and you are free from the habitual contractions of negative emotions.

Millman maintains that we can attain an underlying happiness that is independent of positive or negative circumstances. Although Millman does not prescribe absolute avoidance of expressing negative emotions like Ouspensky, he advocates disconnecting habitual expression and identification from the emotions and events of our lives. He writes in *No Ordinary Moments,* "True happiness is the ability, developed over time and with practice, to radiate positive energy regardless of external *or* internal circumstances.... Over time, I've found that beneath these emotions [anger, sadness] I still feel an undercurrent of happiness that cannot be diminished by whatever drama I'm going through at the personality level."[19] Both Millman and Castaneda say that one manifestation of the warrior spirit is in being happy for no apparent reason. The happiness of the ordinary person is tied to the events of her day. Warriors generate their own happiness.

Imagination

Imagination, properly used, can spark creativity and allow ideas and possibilities to form that we have never experienced. Imagination, in the sense that Ouspensky used the term, is a major power leak. It is important to understand how Ouspensky used the term. The principal question he applied to imagination and all other functions was, "Is it under our control or not?"[20] By Ouspensky's definition, imagination is out of control and is, in fact, controlling the one who imagines. It is possible to allow this form of pseudo-thinking to drain away personal power in a variety of ways, each characterized by nonproductive mental activity that distracts us from the here and now.

We can direct imagination toward the outer world or toward ourselves. We can imagine many scenarios that conflict with what has actually taken place. How often have we indulged in imagining outcomes based on such statements as "If only I had said ... If I knew then what I know now ... If I had it to do over...." Usually the ensuing fantasies are the only consequences of these speculations, and if given a chance to do it over, people usually act automatically in the same way as before.

Similarly, imagination is the primary vehicle for worrying. Worry is a type of imagination in which negative outcomes are viewed and reviewed with a wide range of negative emotions and stress responses accompanying the imagination. The field of psychophysiology has demonstrated that the parts of the brain that activate stress respons-es such as muscle tension, glandular secretions, cardiovascular changes, and increased flow of gastric juices respond to imaginal input just as they respond to information coming directly through the senses. It is quite possible to worry oneself sick, and when this occurs the pow-er leak of imagination has serious health consequences.

When directed toward oneself, imagination concocts a host of non-existent states, non-existent possibilities and non-existent powers. People imagine that they are awake when they are actually deep in consensus trance. Each imagines that he or she operates from a sin-gle, unified self when really functioning as a ship of fools. They imag-ine they have the power to direct the course of their lives when they actually live under the law of accident. These applications of imagi-nation create the illusion, or delusion, that we are much more devel-oped than we are. This is a grandiose misappraisal.

Remember that the key test here is whether the function is under your control—really under your control, not just imagined to be. There are ways of thinking hypothetically that do not constitute imag-ination because they lead to productive changes. Feldenkrais summed this up by saying, "Thinking means new ways of acting."[21] If you use your powers of imagery to rehearse and invent new ways of coping with certain situations and then actually do things differently, you are not imagining in the way being discussed here. If, however, your imaginal processes do not lead to new ways of acting, you are not thinking. You are engaging in what Feldenkrais called *cerebration.* Cer-ebration is a type of cognitive, neurological activity that takes place in closed loops within the nervous system, meaning they have no outlet in terms of action. Unless your thought processes orient to new options, you are not really thinking. If you are choosing to think in pointless loops you may be leaking power, whether your activity is under control or not.

On the other hand, if your thinking processes are under your con-trol and lead to new ways of acting, they can be very valuable. Creative visualization, inventive thinking, and problem solving are all ways in which imaginal processes are useful. The ability to think in "what if" terms in order to choose courses of action is very adaptive because doing so enables you to consider possible consequences without having to suffer them. When you use imaginal processes positively, power is directed toward action. Warriors use these actions according to their strategy for living, and power is used productively. Imagination, or cerebration, dissipates power and can lead to deterioration of health and curtailing of growth.

Cease Imagination

Again awareness is the first tool to be used in plugging a power leak. Being aware of when you are imagining is necessary if anything is to be done about it. It is also important to distinguish between time spent in imagination and time spent in thinking. One important test for whether your thought process is imagination or not is to determine if you initiated the particular line of mental activity, or if you suddenly found yourself caught up in it. Another important factor to know is whether any particular mental activity leads to new ways of acting. You will recall that this was Feldenkrais' test for differentiating between real thinking and cerebration.

Warriors realize that both thinking and imagining are activities that they themselves do, and the primary difference is that imagination is an automatic, habitual process, while thinking is controlled and productive. Thinking and imagining can be viewed as actions. The warrior has the power to choose between them, or to choose to do or not to do either of them. Once awareness tells you that you are imagining, you have the opportunity to choose to discontinue imagining or to choose some other activity.

There are some specific tools that can be used to learn to curtail imagination. The discipline of meditation, the process of self-remembering, and any means of training yourself to focus attention will help diminish imagination. As Ouspensky says, "If attention is fixed on something, imagination stops."[22] Learning to stay focused on what is present—whether it is an internal process like deliberate, creative visualization, or an external event in the world—will help free the warrior from the power leak of imagination by creating a state of awareness that is incompatible with imagination. To cease imagination completely is a most difficult task, one that perhaps only a master warrior could accomplish, but anyone interested in progressing on this path can develop enough control to begin diverting power and time from imagining to true thinking and action.

Hope

In his article "Dreams In The Warrior's Wake," Dennis Leri tells how hope depletes personal power. He writes:

> The warrior dreams of a hopeless world. The average person hopes all along that things will change. They hope and pray endlessly for the coming to pass of what they know or what others have known. Their faces are turned away from the Openness, away from space, away from the unknown. Hope blinds and condemns the hopeful to a C+ existence at best. Hope is at war with perception, with action, with the means whereby one can actually wrest with their own hands their own destiny.[23]

Leri has recognized that a warrior cannot afford to lose power by engaging in processes that interfere with her ability to perceive her surroundings and to take the path of action. He has pointed out that to hope things will become other than they are is folly and immobilizes us by luring us into a process of imagination. Once we begin to imagine in ways that do not lead to new action and to expanding awareness of self and surroundings, power is squandered. The situation that we so hoped would change either does not change or it changes in a way totally unrelated to how we hoped it would. Such an outcome is likely to spark another outburst of hope, with much the same result as before.

Hope, as Leri portrays it for the average person, distracts people from the here and now. To hope in this way would prevent a warrior from being effective in dealing with whatever situation is currently at hand. The warrior must deal with the flux of events; to divert her power into hoping things change to suit her wishes will diminish effectiveness, not to mention possibly putting her in peril.

It has become fashionable to practice affirmations as a way of influencing events and creating one's own reality. People also use prayer for these ends as they petition higher beings to intercede on their behalf. Nevertheless, people usually use prayer and affirmations very much like Leri describes them using hope, and the results are similar.

Since people usually pray as an act of hope instead of an act of power, most prayers and affirmations are ineffective. The Gurdjieff work explains why.

Recall that Gurdjieff pointed out that few people have a central "I." This means that many subpersonalities are active, and while one of them may be praying for something to happen, others may hold very different intents. This means the person is not praying with her whole being, but only with a part of herself. Such a prayer is usually canceled out, because the other aspects of false personality pursue quite different intentions through the day. One needs a consistent desire congruently integrated into one's whole being.

Internal inconsistency makes prayers and affirmations ineffective in another way. Tart points out that how we live our lives often negates our prayers. A person who prays at night for peace may engage in conflict all day long. The day's behavior actually acts as a different prayer, whether the person intends it so or not. What we hold on our minds and express in our actions has great influence over our lives. As Gurdjieff said, "Your being attracts your life."[24]

We can use affirmations and prayer effectively. In effective prayer, one prays with a conscious intensity as well as consistent desire. The intensity can be reached during extraordinary circumstances, such as emergencies, when one asks for help; but even if the help is granted, we fade back into our usual scattered way of being after the emotions of the moment recede. We need to be able to muster intensity in a volitional way that does not require temporary emergencies. In explaining how a conscious person with this capacity would pray, Tart writes he would be effective "if he prayed from his more integrated and constructive subpersonalities or from his essence, better yet." He continues with, "Remembering yourself while you pray is the most effective of all."[25]

Praying consciously in the way Tart proposes is similar to meditation and involves a change in one's psychophysical state, focusing consciousness in a powerful way. Such a prayer petitioning a higher being, or higher level of being, may very well be effective. From the ordinary state of consciousness this "magic" is not possible, but from a certain altered state it is.

Prayers and affirmations can be useful and effective, but most of the time they are little more than hope. Hope will divert one from perceiving and acting and is therefore ineffective at anything except to drain personal power and create illusions. Effective prayer and affirmation require a desire congruently experienced throughout one's being and the ability to be consciously intense.

Letting Go of Hope

Since hope is a special form of imagination, many ideas and procedures discussed in the last section apply to letting go of hope. This form of imagination is primarily concerned with imagining things are other than they are. Therefore, the best antidotes are acceptance and awareness. The warrior chooses to be aware of herself and her world and tries to free herself from judgmental imaginings and evaluations. In other words, she accepts what she finds neither wishing it were different, nor hoping it will magically change. If she decides to change things, she does it. She does not just hope and wish.

Don Juan taught Castaneda about another variety of acceptance—accepting one's fate, rather than struggling with trying to change one's nature or destiny. Don Juan said, "The warrior takes his lot, whatever it may be, and accepts it in ultimate humbleness."[26] To do so allows her to proceed without regrets, or as don Juan revealed, "A warrior's joyfulness comes from having accepted his fate, and from having truthfully assessed what lies ahead of him."[27] Accepting her fate allows a warrior to proceed with the direction of her life without wasting power resisting who and what she is and without hoping and striving to change the line of her destiny. Chivas Irons colorfully reported resisting his fate and, as Michael Murphy chronicled it, "Once he made the decision to accept these disparate leadings he was no longer 'a chameleon on a tartan plaid' responding to every situation and impulse that came his way."[28] Acceptance, awareness, and the general curtailing of imagination can go far in plugging the power leak of hope and can allow the warrior to get on with her quest for an impeccable life.

Other Power Leaks

We have not exhausted the list of power leaks. There are many more, such as excessive talking and excessive thinking, but by now the reader should have the knowledge needed to find power leaks and understand how they work. The types of power leaks we have discussed are not discreet, as there is often overlap among them. Keep this in mind as you search out ways in which your personal power oozes away from you. Also, remember that a particular function does not always represent a power leak. One key concept to remember is that warriors seek to awaken from the ordinary state of consensus trance and escape from mechanicalness, and anything that promotes mechanicalness is very likely to be a power leak. Another general guideline to determining if a function is a power leak is to apply Ouspensky's question, "Is it under our control or not?" If it is not, the function is probably a power leak.

Once the warrior begins to reclaim personal power from power sinks and stem the flood of power through the sieve of power leaks, she is living more and more impeccably. Impeccability grants her the power to tackle the warrior's quest—to cross the border between the known and the unknown in search of an expanded relationship with the universe and even more personal power. Now let us find out more about the unknown and how to hunt power there.

Chapter Seven

The Unknown

The unknown is both mysterious and familiar to the warrior. Because of his flexibility and versatility, the warrior functions well in the everyday realm, but unlike most ordinary people, warriors actively seek the adventuresome realm of the unknown. It is this seeking that in large part defines what a warrior is. Not content to rest in the arena of what is only functional, and apparently safe and secure, the warrior seeks to expand perception in a lifelong quest for knowledge and a larger perspective of the world. The warrior is drawn to the unknown like a flower opening to the morning sun. Seeking the unknown is a tropism for the warrior, an innate tendency to respond to the unknown with a sense of awe and yearning, a desire so strong that the warrior is willing to yield to the discipline and preparation that is necessary to undertake his quest.

Although a specific definition of the unknown will always elude us there are ways of talking and thinking about it that yield a useful framework and give a taste of what is out there. "Everything that surrounds us is an unfathomable mystery," writes Castaneda in *The Eagle's Gift*. "We must try to unravel these mysteries, but without hoping to accomplish this."[1]

To be comfortable with this mysticism requires a warrior's spirit, an open mind, sufficient personal power, and the desire to explore beyond the everyday borders of the known. Don Juan explained to Castaneda that although the unknown is veiled from man, it is within his reach. It is the warrior's task to reach into the domain of mystery, to extend his hand without knowing ahead of time what is there to grasp.

Though the unknown is a mystery, it is something that can be assimilated by the warrior. Still, there is a realm beyond the unknown that is even more enigmatic. Again, don Juan explains, "The unknown becomes the known at a given time. The unknowable, on the other hand, is the indescribable, the unthinkable, the unrealizable. It is something that will never be known to us, and yet it is there, dazzling and at the same time horrifying in its vastness."[2] Similarly, the cosmology of the Fourth Way schools of Gurdjieff, Ouspensky, and Bennett describes different levels of organization of the universe that lead ultimately to *The Absolute,* which is so far beyond the experience and mind of man that it is forever indecipherable.

So we have defined three realms. The known includes all that is currently known by an individual. Some elements of the unknown for one person might have been in the known for someone else for a long time. All that one does not currently know is held in either the unknown, a domain of inexhaustible scope with elements he might eventually comprehend, or in the unknowable. The unknown is the mysterious realm where the warrior travels in quest of knowledge; but if the warrior encounters the unknowable, disastrous results may ensue. One must have great power and impeccability, beyond what is needed to withstand the journey into the unknown, to withstand the presence of the unknowable. Given the nature of these mysteries, the anxiety that develops when one steps beyond the borders of the familiar world is easy to understand. This is why the warrior must pursue impeccability, the development of fearlessness, adherence to discipline, and the acquisition of power to make and survive his journey.

Beyond this delineation of domains that define the universe of knowledge, it is possible to construct models of reality that enable us to talk meaningfully about both the known and the mysteries of the unknown. One of these models comes from the science of modern physics and is expressed eloquently in the writings of David Bohm.

Bohm describes the universe as being composed of two orders, the explicate and the implicate. The explicate is the ordinary reality that is perceived in relatively similar ways by most people. It is the reality of things—things that have an objective form, things that feel solid, things that seem to exist independently of human beings and can be verified by both senses and consensus.

On the other hand, there is the implicate order. This is a great cosmic soup in which things have no form, and thus are not things at all. This is a mathematical domain in which reality does not yield to the senses, but exists as endless probability. Entire worlds, entire universes can coalesce from this soup, and it is from this source that our own world of form has arisen. Any changes in our objective, ordinary reality will likewise arise from this cauldron of probability. The implicate order is like an infinite, supersaturated solution from which any number of precipitates could crystallize into any type of explicate form that is allowable under the laws by which the universe operates. Another way of saying this is explicate reality is enfolded in the implicate order and unfolds from it.

This theory has definite parallels in the modern mythology of warriorship, and to understand the warrior's journeys into the unknown it is useful to find common ground between the scientific and mythical understandings of the way reality is constructed. Let us return to Castaneda.

Don Juan described to Castaneda the difference between the *tonal* and the *nagual*. The tonal correlates to the known and includes the world of objects as they are reported ordinarily by the senses. Yet this a limited view of reality, as there is much more to the world than this ordinary version. Our ability to apprehend the world is restricted by something called the bubble of perception, and Castaneda's tutoring in sorcery was, in large part, designed to burst his bubble of perception and let him engage non-ordinary reality. This took him into the unknown, into the realm of the nagual.

Once a warrior enters the nagual he must immediately begin the process of returning to the tonal, because to slip too far into the nagual would be very harmful, leading to the warrior's death or derangement. The amount of personal power a warrior has determines the depth of confrontation with the nagual he can survive.

Bohm's implicate order and Castaneda's nagual are similar in that both are impossible to describe because the description must be done by thinking, and thought can only apply in the domains of the tonal and the explicate order of that which is manifest. Bohm says, "Thought cannot grasp that which is. And any attempt to grasp that which is engages us in serious self-deception which confuses everything . . . it [thought] does not attempt to grasp the questions which are beyond it."[3]

In *Tales of Power*, don Juan insists, "The nagual is the part of us for which there is no description—no words, no names, no knowledge." Castaneda replies to him by naming a variety of things that he guesses would be synonymous with the nagual—mind, soul, thoughts, heaven, energy, immortality, God—and don Juan says that these cannot be the nagual, because the tonal encompasses everything we think, and Castaneda's guesses are all things of which he thinks. When Castaneda explains that to him God is everything, don Juan refutes him with, "No. God is only everything you can think of."[4] In this way he reminds Castaneda that any concepts he holds are limited by the finite scope of his thoughts.

You can see that even this discussion about the unknown is in danger of being very misleading, for we are on the horns of a dilemma. The more we think about the unknown, the more we materialize the "thought." The more crystalline the thought becomes, the more it is removed from the unknown. It is important to remember that the point of this chapter is to lead us in a direction for exploration and perhaps to pacify our rationality that seeks to conceptualize everything and often tries to hold us back until it has some degree of clarity of thought. Nevertheless, nothing that is written here and nothing that is thought about in response to this writing will serve to contact the unknown. In the words of don Juan, "The nagual . . . can be witnessed, but it cannot be talked about."[5] The *tao* that can be spoken is not the eternal Tao, according to Taoist religious teaching. All we are doing here is talking about concepts of the unknown, not about the unknown itself.

Even so, the concepts prove to be very interesting, and there must be some value in discussing them or don Juan and Socrates would not have taken so much time in doing so with their apprentices. Let us return to physics and deal with the concepts in a slightly different way.

One of the most successful theories of modern physics is the theory of quantum mechanics, an explanation of which is far beyond the scope of this book. There is a thought-provoking problem in quantum mechanics that is often posed to students. It is called the dilemma of "Schroedinger's Cat." This problem is clearly discussed in a delightful book that presents physics in an understandable way for those without much mathematical knowledge. In *The Dancing Wu Li Masters*, Gary Zukav presents the problem like this:

> A cat is placed inside a box. Inside the box is a device which can release a gas, instantly killing the cat. A random event (the radioactive decay of an atom) determines whether the gas is released or not. There is no way of knowing, outside of looking into the box, what happens inside it. The box is sealed and the experiment is activated. A moment later, the gas either has been released or has not been released. The question is, without looking, what has happened inside the box. According to classical physics, the cat is either dead or it is not dead. All that we have to do is to open the box and see which is the case. According to quantum mechanics, the situation is not so simple.[6]

The solution to the problem of "Schroedinger's Cat" depends upon the interpretation of quantum mechanics to which you subscribe. If you are interested in a discussion of the various interpretations, read Zukav's book. For our purposes, though, we will deal with one particular theory called the Copenhagen Interpretation.

This theory views the cat's existence very differently from a commonsense approach. It is not so much that the cat is either alive or dead, but that inside the box the cat's existence is defined by a mathematical idea called a wave function that contains one possibility—that the cat is alive—and another possibility—that the cat is dead. Until the box is opened and an observation made, both possibilities exist. One might say that the cat is either both alive and dead, or that it is neither alive nor dead, until the box is opened. It is the act of observation that defines reality.

Let's look at the wave function more closely. It also could be called a probability function because it represents the probability values for the cat's chances of living or dying. When such functions are graphically represented they look something like a pile of sand. The more sand there is under a given point, as defined by the three-dimensional coordinates, the greater the probability of a particular event occurring. But, nothing has happened yet! All possible events exist only as their particular probability value and do not take on form in ordinary reality until some observation is made. Everything that is possible has some probability value, some chance of becoming actual, and these chances vary according to the natural laws operating.

If you are going to draw a card from a deck of playing cards, the probability of drawing the ace of spades is one in fifty-two, the same as for any other card. This probability exists in its mathematical form before you draw, but you will not know which probability you have actualized until you draw a card and look at it. Mathematically, the act of making an observation and actualizing a given event is called collapsing the wave function. This removes the event from the realm of probability because it is now in the realm of certainty. When one possibility becomes a certainty, its probability value is one hundred percent which collapses all other possibilities, reducing their chances of occurring to zero. Once you draw the ace of spades there is no chance that it is the queen of diamonds.

The significance of this theory lies in its insistence that reality is defined by the act of observation. The wave function is much like Bohm's implicate order. It is a way of describing the cosmic soup that underlies that which is manifest. The universe exists in a totally incomprehensible way, and it is only made comprehensible by an act of comprehending. When we observe, we literally create the world in our minds and with our minds. This is how we make maps in NLP terms. Maps are made from sensory observations, but the territory is the wave function.

For the sake of accuracy let me say that most physicists believe that such theories as the Copenhagen Interpretation apply to the microscopic world of subatomic particles. The application of those theories to the macroscopic world in which we live has yet to be proven, and thought exercises such as Schroedinger's Cat are designed to illustrate points rather than present the theory in detail. To extend the idea that reality is constructed by an act of perception, we will look at a biologically oriented approach described by Feldenkrais, a physicist, and we will let Castaneda lead us into the macroscopic.

Feldenkrais believed that an important function of nervous systems is to create order out of chaos. Where no order is apparent, one will be imposed by the nervous system. Since humans have highly developed nervous systems, we are very skilled at creating order, which is another way of saying that we are good at collapsing wave functions. This act creates a world that we take to be reality. In other words, with our nervous systems we create the known, and because of the manifest and crystalline nature of our thoughts about the known, we usually fall into the trap of thinking that what we see is the only reality possible. It is imperative that warriors avoid this trap because it prevents all contact with the unknown and leads to a brittle state of mind that requires constant expenditure of vast amounts of energy to defend a particular definition of reality.

One reason the Copenhagen Interpretation of quantum mechanics is so interesting is that Castaneda's system is very similar. The wave function has a direct parallel in what Castaneda calls the Eagle's emanations. In *The Fire from Within* don Juan asserts, "Everything is made out of the Eagle's emanations."[7] The Eagle is not really an eagle but is called that because of the way it appears to seers. It is the giver of awareness and the controlling power behind the destinies of living things. From this source, whatever it is, come emanations that compose the world. These emanations apparently have no form as such and are the ingredients of the cosmic soup that lies behind our ordinary reality.

As in quantum mechanics and the implicate order theory, reality is formed from this cosmic soup by acts of perception. Castaneda discusses this in many places in his writings and the message is always the same—we create the world by perceiving, and we learn what to perceive. Our perceptions, though, are limited by our backgrounds. As we grow up we learn a description of the world, and in adopting this description we make the assumption that the description is reality.

We solidify this assumption as we talk to ourselves, constantly rein-forcing the description until we are certain that nothing exists except reality as we perceive it. Don Juan would say this is a grave error indeed, because this type of ordinary reality is only one version of what we could perceive. His training of Castaneda was primarily focused on helping him perceive a more extended range of reality. To extend the range of perception beyond the described and known real-ity, Carlos had to enter the unknown, since everything that lies beyond what we are trained to perceive as real is in the unknown. The rela-tionship between what we sense and the vast possibilities of the Eagle's emanations is recounted by don Juan when he says, "Something is out there affecting our senses. This is the part that is real. The unreal part is what our senses tell us is there."[8] If he were a physicist, don Juan would be saying that the true reality is the implicate order while the explicate order is transitory.

This system includes a theory about the mechanism of perception that is recounted in several of Castaneda's books. In don Juan's scheme of things, human beings can appear as luminous beings of energy, and there is a certain structure in this luminous body called the *assem-blage point.* This structure is responsible for perception of the world and of oneself. Don Juan says, "The fixation or the movement of the assemblage point is all there is to us and the world we witness, what-ever that world might be."[9] The complex process in which the assem-blage point functions is described in Castaneda's writings, but for our purposes here we note that the assemblage point specifies the range of the Eagle's emanations that can be perceived at a given time.

If the assemblage point moves to another position in the luminous body a different range of the Eagle's emanations can be perceived, which gives the warrior access to the unknown. If the point moves only a small distance, there may be considerable overlap between the world we perceive ordinarily and the new one. If the assemblage point moves a great distance from its customary position, an entirely new world might emerge. Castaneda often found himself in extremely dif-ferent, otherworldly surroundings, and it was the shift in the assem-blage point location that allowed him to perceive the new worlds. There were times when the new world was similar to this one, but it was populated with strange creatures. This too was a result of a shift of the assemblage point.

For most people the assemblage point finds its standard location fairly early in life. Throughout the course of our education, when we are given the "correct" description of the world, the assemblage point becomes more or less fixed in a given position. This position limits what we can perceive because all the Eagle's emanations that produce other worlds are outside the range of what can be assembled in our minds. As we develop an internal dialogue we constantly reinforce our ordinary description of reality and keep the assemblage point moored in an habitual location. All we can perceive is the known.

Since the world description in a given culture is relatively homogeneous, members of that culture experience reality in similar ways. Each culture educates its members, installing in them a common world view and a range of perception accepted as reality. This allows us to gain consensual validity for our view of reality from people around us who have assemblage points in similar locations. However, people with greatly different experiential backgrounds may differ from us significantly in terms of what they believe is real. Descriptions of reality vary among cultures, so it could be argued that the position of assemblage points among Balinese is different from the position among Eskimos. Therefore, they would not necessarily validate each other's world view. The differences between cultures show that reality is arbitrary and not an unquestionable fact.

The notion of an assemblage point is unique to Castaneda's writings. It may exist as described, or it may not. Either way we are clearly talking about how our way of perceiving the world changes. Under the influence of certain stimuli we see things differently and interpret the world unconventionally. This is a shift in perception and often corresponds to special states of consciousness. Perception can be altered by many factors, such as beliefs, social influences, drugs, fasting, prolonged exertion, and expectation. When such alterations occur we really do see and experience the world in unusual ways. We may see things that we missed in other states of perception, even if they are quite ordinary things. Entering a quiet state, for example, can enable us to be aware of sounds that escaped our awareness previously.

Apparently we can detect a certain range of stimuli in each state of consciousness and perception that we enter. Don Juan would explain this by repeating that each location of the assemblage point can capture only a selected range of the Eagle's emanations, and to expand or alter that range the assemblage point must shift. The construct of an assemblage point is not necessary to explain how shifts in perception occur, but it does offer an explanatory model that has great pragmatic value for warriors who seek the unknown and must change their way of perceiving.

As explained previously, warriors must find a way to detect and assemble a novel range of stimuli to enter the unknown. Using Castaneda's construct of the assemblage point provides an easy way to talk about this process, but how does one go about moving the assemblage point and changing perception?

Don Juan's answer is power. A great deal of personal power, a great deal of energy, is required to shift the assemblage point voluntarily from its otherwise rigid position. The usual position defines the everyday world—and even warriors can have a hard time giving up the standard definition. Castaneda's first book, *The Teachings of Don Juan*, contains extensive descriptions of how don Juan gave Carlos power plants, strong hallucinogenic substances, to move his assemblage point and propel him into the unknown of non-ordinary reality. Later don Juan explained that hallucinogens are unnecessary, but they had been expedient in Carlos' case because of his extreme stubbornness in clinging to his habitual definition of reality. After much training, Carlos could enter the unknown because he had acquired enough personal power to make his assemblage point shift and to maintain the altered position for a sufficient length of time. With enough personal power, warriors make shifting the assemblage point a fluid operation and can move from the tonal to the nagual and back at will.

The similarities between scientific and mythological views of how reality is constructed and defined are very interesting and provocative. Both specify that acts of perception or observation manifest reality. You may take your choice of whether to describe this as collapsing a wave function or assembling the Eagle's emanations. Both theories present abstractions that provide models for dealing with concepts of reality, but are themselves removed from reality. What is important from a warrior's standpoint is that the unknown is the source of greater knowledge and that knowledge can be claimed as power. To seek the unknown is the warrior's tropism, and to walk his path requires him to aspire to a much broader perception and understanding of reality than that possessed by ordinary people. The freedom that comes from succeeding in his quest to contact the unknown fulfills the warrior's destiny.

Chapter Eight

Hunting Power

IN LEARNING TO live an impeccable life the warrior plugs as many power leaks as completely as she can. With the power that is saved and the energy that is freed she can hunt additional power deliberately and effectively. To hunt power successfully, the warrior must venture into the realm of the unknown, the very lair of power.

The Threshold

Along with her impeccable style of living, the warrior's relationship with the unknown sets her apart from ordinary people. When people without the warrior's abilities, perspectives, and experiences cross the threshold of the unknown their responses are confusion, fear, possibly panic, and usually retreat. The warrior welcomes the contact with the unknown as an opportunity for learning and for increasing personal power. The average person seeks the comfort of what she already knows and abhors the confused feelings that come from entering the unknown realms. The warrior, on the other hand, not only tolerates the unknown, but seeks it. Our working definition of a warrior is an impeccable hunter of personal power. The source of greater personal power being the unknown, the warrior knows that she must cross the threshold. She cannot hunt more personal power in the known. Her strategy in dealing with the known is to become more impeccable. In the unknown she must employ flexibly a different and crucial set of skills.

Knowing What To Do

Dennis Leri calls the category of skills that make up the warrior's strategy for coping with the unknown *knowing what to do when you don't know what to do.* Leri's idea forms a core around which a package of specific skills orbits. The skills involved are embedded in the warriorship teachings, but knowing what to do when you don't know what to do boils down to this cluster:

1. Accepting the confusion and uncertainty as signs you are in the unknown without indulging in confusion, panic, or automatic retreat.
2. Shifting to higher levels of awareness of self and surroundings.
3. Relying on internal rather than external reference points. This amounts to trusting personal power.
4. Not-doing of habitual responses.

Since this bundle of skills is so crucial in the hunt for power, let us pursue each of these points. The first is fairly straightforward. The feelings that come from crossing the threshold between the known and unknown are similar from person to person. The difference separating warriors from non-warriors lies in the interpretation of and responses toward those feelings. The ordinary person interprets the feelings as dangerous and unpleasant and then tries to minimize them by returning to the known or by manipulating the situation to create an illusion that they are actually on familiar ground. They indulge in the confusion, focus on it, and complain to themselves or others how unpleasant it is. Magnifying the unpleasant aspects repels them from the unknown, and they never learn what to do when they don't know what to do. Their attention narrows and they turn away from the open spaces of the unknown. Essentially, their quest is for comfort instead of personal power and knowledge. Their strategy is to minimize change.

To warriors, confusion and uncertainty are signs that they have crossed the threshold into the unknown, and instead of indulging in the feelings, they remember that they know what to do when they don't know what to do. They are hunters and they know it is time for the hunt.

The second part of the meta-strategy for knowing what to do when you don't know what to do is to shift to a higher level of awareness. On this side of the threshold everything is unfamiliar. Even if something appears familiar it is better not to assume that it is. This will be determined later. For now the warrior's task is to gather information upon which to choose courses of action. The warrior shifts to a higher level of awareness of self and surroundings. She becomes aware of her physical, attitudinal and, emotional responses. She opens herself to receive impressions from the outside. This is usually done in an alert but relaxed way. Becoming tense will lock up parts of her nervous system and those parts are available for nothing else at that moment. Concentration is best avoided. Concentration involves a centralizing of attention, like looking down a tunnel, focusing only on the speck of light at the end. You need to be aware of the periphery also, so an expanded kind of attention is needed.

You can demonstrate this physically for yourself. Imagine information is like seeds blown on the wind toward you. Concentration is like extending your arms in front of you with your hands close together. With your attention on the narrow gap between your hands, your arms will deflect any seeds that blow to you, except the ones that happen to have just the right trajectory to enter the space between your fingertips. If this is your manner of harvesting the free information all around, you will be impoverished and have a very restricted impression of the surroundings.

Now, what if you open your arms wide, like a satellite dish antenna? You will gather many more seeds, especially if you turn to harvest them from many directions. This is inclusive, expansive attention and it has a different application than concentration, which is an important skill for other times.

Once, at a beginners' rock climbing class, I saw this difference employed by the instructor. He told the students that when they felt stuck on the rock and did not know how to proceed they should open their attention to allow the rock to reveal its secrets. Doing so, they would be surprised to find hand and foot holds poping up as if a cloak had been lifted from them. When the students managed to shift their attention to let the rock yield its secrets, their tension level lowered, their fear began evaporating, and they were soon able to solve the climbing problem. If they used the same type of attention and awareness as they did in the beginning, they often became immobile and terrified. On the rock, or anyplace else in the unknown, the warrior must expand her awareness so she can gather the seeds and secrets of this new place. Alert. Relaxed. Open. Patient.

The third aspect of knowing what to do in the unknown is shifting to internal reference points. The known is filled with familiar reference points and the space is striated, that is, lined and partitioned, in a way that one can recognize the right direction to go and the right way to act. In other words, you know your place. In the unknown, though, there are no familiar reference points. If there were, you would still be in the known. Here in the unknown, the only familiar thing is yourself. If you continue to be aware of your internal landscape and trust the intuitive decisions you make in response to it, you have the best chance of succeeding with your hunt. As your heightened awareness brings you more and more data about the surroundings, you will become more and more able to act intuitively. This is really a matter of personal power. The more power you have, the more capable you are. The warrior will trust in her personal power at this point because she has nothing else to go on. In the movie Star Wars, Luke Skywalker turned off the computer of his star fighter at the most critical moment, responding to his internal teacher's voice that told him to trust his feelings.

You can capture something of the flavor of this yourself by doing an exercise Dennis Leri has used with Feldenkrais Trainees. You need to go to a large room, park, field, or any other space with clearly defined boundaries and angles. Since most such spaces tend to be rectangular, let us proceed as if you have found yourself a large, rectangular space and, to simplify the instructions, envision the space being oriented to the four directions like a map. Now, go to the exact northwest corner of the space. Then go to the other three corners exactly. Pay attention to how you know that you are there. What evidence do you accept?

Now, find the exact center of the space. How do you know when you are there? Do you rely on the same proportion of external and internal information as you did to locate the corners? Are you as certain of your precision in finding the center as you were in the corners?

In Leri's Feldenkrais training, a small group of students was given this task and their responses were very typical. In finding the corners they relied extensively on the external references of the walls of the room. Of course, there was some internal signal, some feeling in the body, that said essentialy, "That's it!" Most of the students' aware-ness was external, however, and they laughed and joked their way through this part of the exercise because the external lines made it so easy. Consensus of the group members about their accuracy in finding the corners was quickly obtained.

Finding the exact center of the gymnasium, though, produced a dramatic change. Here the walls were much less relevant. The stu-dents had to visualize their own lines internally and imagine where they intersected. Getting the internal "That's it!" signal took several adjustments of position. That internal signal became more important evidence of precision than the external walls. At a certain point each person had to determine that they had actually found the exact center, and they determined that by finally trusting their internal signal. Pre-dictably, group consensus was much more difficult, as some trusted their internal reference points more than others.

In the unknown there may or not be walls. There may be angles, but they might be different than the ones you are used to. As a warrior, your awareness of external data is heightened, but you will rely on your internal reference points more, patiently trusting your personal power to provide the best choices possible for you when the time comes to act.

The fourth part of this package is not-doing habitual responses. In the unknown the warrior must operate fluidly and flexibly, often inventing actions and responses on the spot. Being stuck in habitual mode, in which certain responses follow certain stimuli, cannot be a part of the hunt. Habitual mode is predictable, and predictability is the characteristic of the hunted rather than the hunter. If the warrior is responding habitually, to what is she responding? Habits are conditioned in the known and the warrior is now in the unknown. If she responds to the unknown situation as if it is the same as the known, her chances for error are very high. Creatively responding to the flux of events is necessary for survival and for the success of the hunt for power.

This group of skills, forming a meta-strategy for dealing with the unknown, is one of the principal distinctions between a warrior and an average person. The warrior knows that once she is in the unknown she does not know what to do. But she does not panic, because she knows what to do when she doesn't know what to do. She knows that she has to be very aware, not interfere with her own abilities by invoking habits or indulging in confusion, and trust her personal power. In doing this the warrior is acting impeccably.

Shifting the Assemblage Point

To hunt power in the unknown, the warrior must be capable of a special accomplishment—the shifting of her assemblage point. As discussed in Chapter Seven, the assemblage point may be a factual, energetic structure like don Juan describes, or it may refer to a process of changing the scope of awareness. Whatever its ultimate nature, we will use the shifting of the assemblage point as a metaphor for talking about altering the range of awareness and perception.

Everyone can shift his or her assemblage point a little, and sometimes it shifts accidentally in response to intense emotions, surprise, or substances. A skilled warrior, though, can move her assemblage point voluntarily a much greater distance, which will allow her to assemble worlds that are either similar to, or greatly different from, what is ordinarily perceived. Castaneda's teaching stories about his encounters with otherworldly beings, extraordinary landscapes, or unusual abilities are stories about the possibilities that can unfold when the assemblage point shifts. With each such encounter more of the possibilities of the universe are available to the warrior. She knows more about how her world works, and her range of responses becomes greater. In short, because she knows more, the warrior can function in a greater diversity of conditions, which means she has more power. She has more power because she has expanded her relationship with the universe.

This ability is related to the process of not-doing. We must realize that perception is an activity of organizing sensory impressions through a lens tempered by past experience and present expectations. Perception is not passive—it is *doing*. If the warrior crosses the frontier into the unknown and begins perceptual doing she will construct another version of the known and her hunt will be finished.

In *Journey to Ixtlan* Castaneda wrote a whole chapter about this kind of not-doing. In that chapter don Juan talks about not-doing as a key factor in accessing the unknown itself. Not-doing, in this sense, is the process through which the warrior creates separate realities. It is resisting the impulse to organize the Eagle's emanations in the usual way. If you can resist *doing*, that is, arranging your perceptions to create a familiar-looking reality, you can open whole new worlds. If you can resist positioning your assemblage point in the habitual location, you can venture farther into the realm of power. After crossing the threshold of the unknown, behavioral not-doing gives you the creativity to deal with what you find there, and perceptual not-doing keeps you from falling back into the known. When your hunt is finished, doing will bring you home.

Don Juan goes on to say that warriors have two rings of power. The first one is innate and gives us the power of doing. It is an enormous power, for out of this we are able to make and hold onto a world that we can share with others. Everyone has this first ring of power and we link ours with the first rings of power of those around us to construct and maintain consensual reality. The second ring is acquired by warriors as they gain more personal power. This ring is the power of not-doing. It permits the warrior to spin another reality from the thread of the universe. With this kind of not-doing, this ability to move the assemblage point from its customary place, the warrior can leave the shackles of consensual reality and open her hunting ground. This means it is possible to find the unknown and hunt power anywhere through the means of not-doing. Don Juan frequently had Carlos train himself in shifting attention and holding alternate perceptions of common things. Often this involved looking at the "negative spaces" of things. Instead of looking at the branches and leaves of a tree, one looks at the shadows and spaces between the branches and leaves.

Artists are very familiar with this trick and it is often used by Feldenkrais practitioners to see the way in which people organize their bodies in posture and action. Taking a walk through your neighborhood, viewing the familiar scenes in terms of negative spaces, will give you a whole new viewpoint and train you in not-doing. The same is true of shifting perceptual foreground and background, so that what you usually see as the important parts of something are relegated to the background and the usual background is brought to the fore. In music you can make the harmony line into the melody and gain a whole new relationship to the music. Even these relatively accessible means of not-doing can open a fertile ground for hunting power and can lead to more creativity and choices.

Point of Entry

In reading the extraordinary teaching stories of Millman and Castaneda, or even Gurdjieff's *Meetings with Remarkable Men,* one can get the impression that a rendezvous with the unknown entails journeys to inaccessible places and encounters with weird people and circumstances. This can lead many would-be warriors to search for the unknown in foreign lands, drug experiences, or obscure rituals. Many others who would like to walk the warrior's path, believing that such extreme points of entry are necessary, never get started. There is no doubt that the mountains of Asia, the deserts of Mexico, the jungles of South America, and the outback of Australia can provide large doses of the unknown for most of us, but it is not necessary to go there to find it. The unknown is just over the border of the known. That border is not geographical. It is a border of consciousness. The only passport you need is the shifting of your assemblage point, and the only currency is personal power.

You can hunt for power in your current circumstances if you are willing to find other possibilities in those circumstances. You have constructed the world you see around you by virtue of your assemblage point. This entails restricting and filtering the massive amount of stimuli that is available, and it entails "collapsing a wave function" and actualizing one set of probabilities out of a virtually limitless number available. Shifting the assemblage point, which really means entering a level of awareness other than the consensus trance of ordinary living, makes more of the non-ordinary potentialities available.

It is tempting to think of the more esoteric experiences described in much of the warrior mythology as somehow being more important than entering seemingly mundane areas of the unknown, but this is not necessarily the case. One person's area of knowledge may be totally unknown to someone else so it is difficult—and perhaps misleading—to consider one person's unknown to be of higher quality than another person's. Wresting with "allies" in the Sonoran Desert is not necessarily further along the evolutionary path than learning the calculus necessary to understand a theory of astrophysics. Neither of these may be more important than learning how to live in a healthy, intimate relationship. The level of esotericism is probably not the best barometer of the value of any confrontation with the unknown.

What matters is that you are willing to cross the boundary at whatever point is needed. Feldenkrais said, "Find your true weakness and surrender to it. Therein lies the path to genius. Most people spend their lives using their strengths to overcome or cover up their weaknesses. Those few who use their strengths to incorporate their weaknesses, who don't divide themselves, those people are very rare. In any generation there are a few and they lead their generation."[1] If you are very good at coping with the unseen forces of the desert but cannot get along in "civilization," you are not embodying the warrior's spirit. Don Juan was equally composed when functioning as a poor Indian in the desert or as a businessman in coat and tie in Mexico City. There are people who adventure into the occult realms not because that area of the unknown has the greatest potential for their development, but because they are avoiding dealing with their weaknesses. Evading one's weaknesses, whether in the domain of the esoteric or exoteric, by avoiding what one cannot do and defending against what one does not know, is the pathway to mediocrity. Surrendering to your weakness and allowing yourself to cross into the unknown at that point is the path to genius and a hallmark of the warrior's spirit.

There are two main feelings that point the way to one's weaknesses—comfort and fear. These can be used as guides for assessing where your weaknesses lie, which can help you find where to cross the border.

Success is one of the main ways people become limited. Once you are successful at something there is a tendency to stay at that level or to rely exclusively on the formula you used to get that success. Success can form habits, and habits can become comfortable. If you find yourself avoiding anything that takes you beyond your comfortable place and comfortable formula for success, chances are you have found your weakness. All it takes is a slight change in context to turn strength into weakness. If you play to your strength even though it does not work when the context changes, or if you refuse to let the context change, you have found a weakness and you can exploit it by surrendering to it and entering the unknown.

Fear is another limiting factor. For most people fear repels them from whatever it is they fear. This is usually because you doubt your capability to handle it or you do not know what to do at all. While you cannot expect yourself to be skilled at everything, as a warrior you must become skilled at things that matter. Weak tennis players often "run around their backhands." This means that they feel much more capable of hitting a forehand stroke and they try to position themselves so they do not have to hit the weak backhand stroke. Sometimes it works, but much more often you just cannot run fast enough to hit the forehand, and your opponent starts to hit to your weak side all the time. If you are a warrior tennis player, surrender to your weakness and learn how to hit the backhand.

The Hunt

But how do encounters with the unknown increase personal power? In hunting power, the warrior aspires to expand her relationship with the universe, which will augment her personal power. Even the titles of Castaneda's early works allude to his growing relationship with the world around him. *The Teachings of Don Juan, A Yaqui Way of Knowledge* describes the early ways in which Castaneda was given experiences to gain more knowledge, knowledge that came from a setting and way of perceiving that was foreign to his Western mentality. *A Sepa-*

rate Reality speaks to the fact that there are worlds around us we do not ordinarily perceive, and it was to those worlds that Carlos was taken in his hunt for power. Only after he was forced by the sheer potency of his experience to admit that there was much he did not know and much his previous background could not explain could Castaneda accept the validity of the alternative realities to which he was exposed.

It is much the same in Millman's teaching stories. Socrates induces experiences and demonstrates abilities outside the norms of Millman's sense of possibility. Those experiences are so vivid and vital that Millman cannot deny them and he has to open his framework of reality. For both Millman and Castaneda, surrendering the illusion that their previously held views are the only reality is necessary to begin the hunt for power. So too with ourselves. Our hunt for power requires this disillusionment.

We can proceed with the hunt once we surrender the illusion of a fixed, external reality whose dimensions we already know. Our degree of impeccability determines where we can hunt and how far afield we can venture. Becoming more impeccable has stemmed the leakage of power and siphoned power out of power sinks. We have more of our basic ration of power available—the personal power we hold already by virtue of having some degree of relationship with the universe. The deeper and broader this relationship becomes, the more power is conferred. With this extra boost of personal power from the unknown, we can function in a greater range of reality and perceive much that we could not perceive before.

Remember, the known is simply one possibility that has been actualized from the enfolded order of the universe; or if you prefer, one of many bands of the Eagle's emanations. To hold the illusion that this band of emanations is the only true reality is a defensive posture that prohibits warriorship. Relinquishing this belief allows us to encounter more bands of emanations, or said another way, to unfold other possibilities from the enfolded order. These other bands of emanations, other probabilities, are our quarry. If we succeed in actualizing other probabilities of perception and action we will have captured more personal power by virtue of having knowledge and capacities for action in a wider territory.

To hunt wild animals or plants the hunter goes into the territory where they live. A novice hunter must make sound choices at this point or her very survival will be compromised. For one thing, she must choose which quarry to hunt. A first-time hunter would be foolish to hunt lions or sharks because she lacks the knowledge and experience necessary in the event the hunter becomes the hunted. A novice also must choose her hunting ground carefully. To begin in the remote wilderness of Alaska or the interior of the Amazon jungle would be a serious mistake. A third important factor involves finding an appropriate guide. Some guides are familiar with some territories but not others. Some guides have good general survival skills and some are highly specialized. The hunter must be honest with herself about her abilities and must choose the quarry, territory, and guide that is most fitting to her abilities and needs.

As the novice hunter progresses in developing her skills of stalking, studying her quarry, travelling in unfamiliar terrain, orienting herself, handling the unexpected, and returning from the hunt, she can move on to other game and enter more remote territory. Once she has the necessary experience and knowledge she can do things that would have been too risky before. The experienced hunter has more power than she did as a beginner, and that power enables her to do things and travel in terrain that is unimaginable for those with less power.

There are two important borders to recognize. The first is the border between the known and the unknown. This is the line that separates stagnation from growth. Stagnated people think they are playing it safe. If you take no chances, you can't get hurt, right? This is correct only if you are numb to the pain and damage of stagnation. To grow is to avoid senility at an early age. DeRopp said there are only two choices in life—to live like a warrior or a slave. Warriors cross the frontier. Gurdjieff wrote in *Life Is Real Only Then, When "I Am"* that life is like a river that forks into two branches—an evolutionary branch and an involutionary branch. Take the involutionary branch and you spend your whole life just meeting the requirements of nature. Like cattle, your energy goes into breeding, raising young, and being a good member of the herd. Take the evolutionary branch and you can grow. You can have something extra in life for yourself that the other people will never have. Warriors run the rapids of the evolutionary branch.

The second important border is out in the unknown somewhere, separating what you have power to do from what you do not. This is the line don Juan referred to when he told Carlos that as soon as warriors enter the nagual they must be aware of how they are going to get back. When a diver enters the water she knows she only has a certain amount of air, and she must know she can get back to the surface before she uses it all. Warriors can tap reserves of power they usually do not use, and when they do so they surpass previous limits and set new personal bests. Still, even these reserves are limited. Once you are running on this power reserve you are in a risky state. You must get back before you run out.

There is a zone between these two borders. Cross the first border or stagnate. Cross the second and you find disaster. How large your zone of exploration is depends on your personal power. Unfortunately, there is no fuel gauge telling you exactly how much power you have. You must be honest and know yourself. Then determine how much to risk. Venturing into the unknown to hunt power must be a reversible operation. Sometimes you will try things you have never tried before. You have to do these things without waffling. You must commit to the actions with the full force of your warrior's spirit. Even so, you want to be able to return.

I've seen some incredible photographs of some of the world's top rock climbers free-soloing amazingly difficult routes in Yosemite National Park. This means they were climbing very exposed rock faces with no ropes or hardware. Their only protection was their skill. Without question, a fall would be fatal. For these people keeping both feet flat on the ground would have been contrary to their warriors' spirits. Staying at a static level of skill without stretching for more ability and more potent experiences would be unthinkable. Failing at a move beyond their ability would be fatal. This illustrates the warrior's problem. You must cross the first border and you must not cross the second—and you cannot tell for sure where those lines are in advance.

Several other people who were not rock climbers looked at these photos and decided the climbers were crazy or suicidal. This would certainly be true for non-climbers. When it comes to climbing they have no skill, no personal power. Free-soloing these routes would be beyond the limits of intermediate climbers also. For these highly advanced, very powerful climbers the routes were not suicidal; they were merely dangerous.

So it is with any venture into the unknown. If you go beyond the limits of your personal power you are at great risk. The warrior must appraise the risk involved and weigh it against the risk of not getting involved. To avoid extending oneself beyond current knowledge and limitations is to run the risk of stagnation and mediocrity. To extend oneself past the range of one's personal power is to invite the risk of exhaustion, madness, or even death.

Thus forays into the unknown are inherently dangerous. They require the warrior to break the first barrier of limitation and tap her reserves, to enter a realm of great uncertainty where she must trust her personal power and rely on internal reference points. Once the first barrier of limitation is broken, the warrior can continue to hunt power, but if her quarry leads her past the second barrier of limitation, her demise may be at hand. Hunting power in the unknown is risky, there is no doubt. Even so, the warrior must go there. She will take the risk and moderate it with her impeccability, discipline, awareness, and personal power.

The Rewards of Personal Power

The reward for taking the risks of these hunts in the unknown is the successful capture of more personal power. This comes about because the warrior claims knowledge from the unknown realms as power. With each journey, the warrior transforms more of the unknown into the known. With this knowledge she is equipped to function more powerfully in life. The most relevant definition of power offered in *Webster's Seventh New Collegiate Dictionary* is the "ability to act or produce an effect."[2] With more power, then, the warrior gains in her ability to act. In Gurdjieff's language, she can escape from the law of accident and be able *to do.* Having more personal power enables the warrior to be more effective in her life, accomplish her intentions, and live strategically.

The Fourth Way schools teach that one must develop both being and knowledge. Being is developed in warriorship by impeccability which requires discipline and mindfulness. Knowledge is attained by taking risky voyages into the unknown. Impeccable living tightens one's life so that power does not leak away. Hunting power in the unknown bestows greater ability to function effectively which means the warrior can manifest her intentions in the world. It is worth the risk, but can be frightening even so. Now let us explore how warriors relate to fear.

Chapter Nine

Fear and Fearlessness

POPULAR WISDOM TELLS us that people naturally fear the unknown. If this is true, then fear will be a major problem for warriors because the unknown is so often their destination. Fear, more than most other feelings, produces indecision, immobility, or panic. This could be fatal for warriors who operate in a realm where they must control their faculties and have many choices available. To make excursions into the unknown, the warrior must come to terms with fear and how he will deal with it. The writers of the warrior mythology address fear from different points of view and offer different advice on dealing with it. In this chapter we will explore the differences and similarities of the various sources and arrive at some conclusions about productive ways of regarding fear and dealing with it in one's life.

The warrior must recognize fear, understand what his fear means, and decide what to do about it. The warrior cannot be a victim of fear and cannot regard it as something that invades him and takes over his emotions. He cannot allow it to dictate feelings and actions. Left unchecked, fear will derail the warrior's strategy and disrupt his acts. All warriors must take a stand with fear and decide how to move beyond it.

In the science fiction book *Dune,* Frank Herbert offers a warrior-ship practice called the "Litany Against Fear." It illustrates the danger of being a victim of fear and offers a strategy for coping with fear when it occurs. The Litany goes as follows:

> I must not fear.
> Fear is the mind-killer.
> Fear is the little death that brings total obliteration.
> I will face my fear.
> I will permit it to pass over me and through me.
> And when it has gone past I will turn the inner eye to see its path.
> Where the fear has gone there will be nothing.
> Only I will remain.[1]

The warrior must be able to act swiftly and decisively, maintaining awareness of the flux of his surroundings. He cannot do this when controlled by fear. The immobilizing influence of fear—the little death—can lead, as Herbert says, to total annihilation. Now let us examine fear and fearlessness from the perspective of writers of the warrior mythology.

Trungpa

Trungpa says fearlessness is living without deception. If one understands the true nature of the world there is no need to deceive others or oneself. This is a difficult position to attain, for one must not only have direct, personal experience of the essence of the world, but must deal with the manifestations of that essence in the phenomenal world without interference of the ego.

Basic Goodness

Basic goodness is the essential, fundamental quality of existence. It is more fundamental than the duality of "good versus bad" and warriors seeking a fearless way of life can sense it. Basic goodness is not relative to something that is bad or something that is less good. It could be termed a natural law, of which Trungpa says, "There is a natural law and order that allows us to survive and that is basically good, good in that it is there and it works and it is efficient."[2] Sunlight and water are good because they are part of this deep natural order, an order in which the light and water fill certain niches and provide certain functions. They are essential components of the way our natural world operates, and therefore they have basic goodness by definition.

To experience fearlessness, the warrior must sense the underlying, fundamental qualities of the natural order through which the world functions. However, he also must sense the presence of basic goodness in himself and other human beings. Rather than judging that certain human attributes are better than others, the warrior in search of basic goodness appreciates the role that all human qualities play in human existence. As Trungpa says, "Human existence is a natural situation, and like the law and order of the world, it is workable and efficient."[3] Even if a person's state is not as enlightened or advanced as it could be, the Shambhala viewpoint requires that the warrior deal with it as it is, without hoping it will become otherwise and without judging his current condition as a failure or shortcoming. Finding basic goodness in people does not mean finding moral perfection. It means appreciating how human faculties and characteristics interact with, and form part of, the working of the world. Trungpa asserts that people have all the faculties they need to live without fighting their world. Seeing the way we are in terms of basic goodness brings home the point that we are well equipped and adequate for the job of surviving and flourishing, if only we can come to know that it is true.

To realize the Shambhala view of basic goodness, we must begin with appreciation. We come to appreciate what we have, and to appreciate ourselves, other people, and the circumstances in which we find ourselves. In learning to appreciate the world in its entirety we can become more open to perceiving the world as it is, without so much interference from our own minds. We decrease how much we habitually filter out of our perceptions and increase the range of our senses.

Appreciation is based on opening to our senses, knowing our hearts, and releasing judgments about what we find there. Our senses are the points of contact with the world around us, and warriors must learn to improve their connection to the world through the senses. Trungpa speaks of going beyond looking to seeing, and likewise, moving from listening to hearing, and from touching to feeling. The warrior learns to trust his senses, although at first relying on senses usually leads to anxiety and retreat. What if we get it wrong? What if we don't like what we see? "But the point is to look properly,"[4] says Trungpa. Look deeper into your world, open to what is there without judgment or retreat, and you will begin to see. Seeing allows you to explore an entire universe and to make discovery after discovery. Through seeing you will really sense the beauty of a sunset; through hearing you will sense the goodness of music; through feeling you will sense fully the textures and contours of the environment. Sensing and curiosity will lead you into a deeper and fuller exploration of the world. Your appreciation of the wonders you find by exploring will lead you to perceive basic goodness.

Beyond sensing the world, the warrior realizes basic goodness by knowing his own heart. Trungpa relates this to the notion of *bodhicitta* from the Buddhist tradition. Translated, this means *awakened heart* and comes from connecting with yourself in an honest examination of whom you are. You look at yourself and into yourself without shying away from what you might find there. Trungpa explains that once you get beyond being embarrassed and worried about knowing yourself, you come to the real nature of your heart. You find that it is soft, tender, and open. This leads you to an unconditioned feeling of sadness that Trungpa believes is the direct antecedent of fearlessness. The sadness comes from the feeling of complete exposure, of being open to experience the world and others directly. Experiencing in such a direct fashion, without creating deceptions designed to shield you from the sadness, is an act of warriorship and an act of fearlessness. "Without that heartfelt sadness," Trungpa says, "bravery is brittle, like a china cup."[5]

His connection with basic goodness allows the warrior to live without deception. Knowing the basic goodness of your nature and your heart means you accept yourself fully, without judgment. Realizing that your essence is basic goodness, you have no need for shyness or embarrassment. You have no need to identify with external things or the trappings of your ego. You have no need to fear who you are.

Knowing the basic goodness of the world means you have no need to deceive yourself or others about reality. There is no need to establish artificial impressions or reference points designed to project or invent any reality other than the one of essential basic goodness. Trungpa reinforces this position by saying, "Experiencing the basic goodness of our lives makes us feel . . . that the world is not a threat. When we feel that our lives are genuine and good, we do not have to deceive ourselves or other people."[6]

Living without Doubt

Believing in basic goodness as a point of doctrine is not good enough. Living fearlessly requires the warrior to be without doubt. He does not doubt his perception of basic goodness, and he trusts himself to act according to his perception. The warrior can drop pretenses and face the shortcomings of his personality without fear only because basic goodness is the fundamental fact of his existence. Likewise, the warrior can interact with other people in a genuine fashion, having no doubt about the outcome ultimately resolving into an expression of basic goodness. The presence of doubt means the warrior is not perceiving basic goodness in the moment.

Imagine trying to resolve a conflict with a friend when you are not sure of the basic goodness of either yourself or your friend. How could you communicate genuinely? The temptation is great to hedge against your doubt by creating some kind of deception or hiding the truth. You will fear that what you say or how you feel will jeopardize the friendship, so you will distort your openness and honesty with each other in an attempt to manipulate the outcome. However, if you are clearly perceiving basic goodness you have no doubt about the outcome being for the best. Your friendship might dissolve, it might strengthen, or it might stay the same. You are willing to accept the reality as it emerges.

Thus, being without doubt allies with detachment from outcome. Attaching to a certain outcome means that you believe that your chosen outcome is necessary and you will selectively perceive only those elements of reality that fit that outcome. Similarly, you will tend to create impressions with your words and actions that are consistent with the specified outcome. You will doubt that the outcome will be acceptable unless you create deception in this way. Trungpa explains one fundamental notion of fearlessness by saying, "You are willing to be awake in whatever situation may present itself to you, and you feel that you can take command of your life altogether, because you are not on the side of either success or failure."[7] Detachment from outcome produces genuine perceptions and actions. Detachment and the absence of doubt let the warrior live without deception and manifest fearlessness.

The Cocoon and the Great Eastern Sun

Trungpa asserts that the common way of dealing with fear is to hide from it and from anything that may remind us of it. To do this we construct a cocoon of familiar habits. Wrapped up in our familiar thoughts, feelings, behaviors, and circumstances, we try to avoid anything new or disturbing. Most of all, we think we are avoiding our own fear. By obsessively insisting on sameness, we think we can evade the things that make us fearful. We think we have made ourselves secure. Trungpa says, "We may think that we have quieted our fear, but we are actually making ourselves numb with fear."[8] Being numb with fear and holding on to the illusion of security, we reject anything new or fresh. Anything other than what is familiar becomes a threat that may expose us to our fear, and we would do anything to dodge that encounter.

The cocoon is the domain of cowardice, and it is a type of dead existence that warriors cannot accept. There is no light or fresh air in the cocoon. There is no contact with the unknown. There is no genuineness. In the warrior's life there comes a time when he revolts against the restrictions of his cocoon, when he feels claustrophobic and begins to crave light, fresh air, and movement. He begins to see the light through the wall of the cocoon, and moving to that point of light, he tears the cocoon open. Through the opening the warrior emerges into the light of the Great Eastern Sun.

The Great Eastern Sun is the Shambhala way of describing a vision of light in which basic goodness is evident. Being in this light allows you to appreciate your existence and to value the world that gives you life. It is a brave and ecological point of view that lets you tune in to the uncontrived order in the world. Great Eastern Sun vision "is based on seeing that there is a natural source of radiance and brilliance in this world—which is the innate wakefulness of human beings."[9] The light of the Great Eastern Sun illumines the warrior's way and shows him the world that was veiled by the cocoon. The warrior uses the light to cleanse himself and the world around him. Basic goodness means that the world and one's self were clean to begin with. Washing away the dirt in your life and cleaning up any mess you have made in the world will uncover the original purity that exists. Therefore, there is nothing to fear, and your fear dissipates in the light of the Great Eastern Sun.

Being in the light makes one's former life in the cocoon repugnant by comparison, but the cocoon has value in an important way. It serves as a point of comparison that keeps us oriented forward. By referring back to the darkness we develop genuine sympathy for our former experience and we understand how that experience can happen to others. We cannot move into the light of the Great Eastern Sun and become complacent there. We cannot escape the darkness and "just bathe in the sun, lying in the sand and stupefying ourselves."[10] That would merely create another cocoon. No, looking back to the darkness, we remember to open ourselves to the continuous journey of warriorship.

The Shambhala teachings show how people try to escape their fear by weaving a cocoon of habitual patterns, but all that accomplishes is to surround themselves with a numbing fear of fear. The warrior must break out of the cocoon and use the light of the Great Eastern Sun to find the basic goodness of himself and the world. From this point of view he is free to develop an organic, uncontrived relationship with the world, appreciating the original purity there. He brushes away the rubbish that he may have put over himself and cleans up any mess he has made so that he may project his basic goodness outward and appreciate the basic goodness that exists in others and the world at large. In so doing the warrior has moved beyond fear and can live without deception.

Millman

Moving beyond fear for Dan Millman means moving into the present, moving into the realm of action. Throughout *Way of the Peaceful Warrior, The Warrior Athlete,* and *No Ordinary Moments,* Millman describes methods of training oneself to sense and focus in the present, to meditate in action. This focus frees the warrior from the illusory world of specific negative emotions, thereby breaking the ability of emotions to drain power from one's actions.

Millman sees negative emotions as the results of uncontrolled thinking. His teacher, Socrates, says, "You have an angry thought bubble up and you *become* angry. It is the same with all your emotions. They're like knee-jerk responses to thoughts you can't control."[11] When a fearful thought presents itself, Millman's advice is to focus on the present and on what must be done, rather than respond to the thought of fear. Even when a dangerous event occurs, such as someone threatening you with a knife, Millman says the warrior will short-circuit the usual tension-fear habit pattern. He counsels, "You don't have to bring a thought or its corresponding tension to *life;* you don't have to dramatize it . . . you do not have to act out the role of someone who is afraid."[12]

Millman is not suggesting that to be a warrior you must rid yourself of all emotions. He does not advocate denial or suppression of emotional awareness. His approach stems from a belief that conditioned, reflexive habit patterns in which a thought, a memory, or a situation compulsively leads you to an emotional response are detrimental. It is not the emotion that is a problem so much as the habit of feeling that emotion whenever a particular stimulus is present. The pattern surfaces whether that emotion fits the current state or not, and regardless of whether the stimulus was a thought or sense perception. These habitual response patterns form through experience, imitation, and programming we get from other people.

Accommodation and Nondramatization

One way Millman recommends of dealing with this problem draws on a principle from his athletic training—the principle of accommodation. He summarizes the principle by saying, "Life develops what it demands," and its corollary, "What is not used becomes obsolete."[13] In other words, the athlete conditions his system by intelligently placing increasing demands on himself to perform in certain ways. The body/mind/spirit responds by accommodating to the demand and improving conditioning and ability. Likewise, when some part or function of the athlete's system goes unused, it atrophies or becomes obsolete. So too with reactive emotional habits. Used and dramatized, they become stronger and more deeply imbedded. When they are short-circuited and not dramatized they weaken. By allowing these unconscious reactions to lose potency, the warrior avoids the tension they produce, and his effectiveness in meeting challenges improves. Millman offers the technique of *nondramatization* as a way of accomplishing this:

> Nondramatization consists of immediate recognition of your psychophysical reality, acknowledging any physical or emotional tension you may feel, and then a conscious letting go: release the tension, breathe slowly and deeply, act positively and effectively. Trust instinct. Feel good, mentally and physically, in spite of whatever negative thoughts may be bouncing around in your head. Negative thoughts don't have to mean negative feelings or tension—*if* you are willing to let go of the thoughts; if you are willing to let yourself feel good in breath and body. That is the essence of nondramatization, and that practice, once proficient, will enable you to transcend the usual knee-jerk reflex of unconscious tension in the face of a difficulty.[14]

Obviously, this is not a recommendation for emotional abstinence. It is a formula for moving beyond habitual fear or other unconscious emotional responses. Rather than employing denial or suppression, Millman offers a positive practice that will allow the warrior to avoid the tension and disruption caused by habitual patterns of emotional response.

Fear of Failure

Millman illustrates how fears are conditioned and relate to not being present in the moment by talking about fear of failure. This fear most often stems from bad experiences and negative feedback from others when we did not succeed. To avoid the unpleasant consequences we try to avoid failure by trying too hard, by avoiding predicaments where we might fail, and by trying to hide failures from others or even from ourselves. But remember, that failure does not exist in the present moment. Our fear of failure relies on anticipation of a negative future outcome or on remembrance of a past outcome. There is no failure in the present, only feedback about whether you are accomplishing your intentions. This feedback is immensely valuable for adjusting your course of action and learning to improve.

In the grip of fear of failure, we no longer use the information as helpful feedback, but as something that must be avoided. Worse, the fear itself produces psychophysical reactions, such as tension, cocontraction of muscle groups, inefficient breathing, and distraction of attention. These responses greatly increase the probability that our fears will come true.

Millman offers two things a warrior can do to deal with fear of failure. First, the warrior interprets the outcomes of his actions as feedback, not failure. This stops him from relating to failure as an enemy and allows him to appreciate the outcome of his acts, whether positive or negative. Millman even advises warriors to fail on purpose sometimes, just to maintain the balanced perspective that success and failure are equally natural. In this way the warrior can disconnect feedback from past learning and extinguish the conditioned fear response.

The main antidote to fear of failure, though, is to stay focused in the present. Pay attention to what you do and if it's working. Focus on the task at hand. Be present. Under these conditions fearful thoughts, anticipations, and recollections will dissipate, leaving a clear view of what you are doing and what must be done. Let your awareness then guide you to more effective and efficient action.

Millman's ideas about fear center on the notion that fearful states generate from one's thoughts, whether about the past or about future possibilities. The warrior moves beyond fear by bringing his awareness fully into the present and focusing on the actions necessary in the moment. Left undramatized, conditioned fear responses will shrink and the warrior will be free of their ability to distract him and drain his power. According to Socrates, "The warrior is *here, now.* Your sorrow, your fear and anger, regret and guilt, your envy and plans and cravings live only in the past or in the future ... when thoughts touch the present, they dissolve."[15] For Millman, moving beyond fear into fearlessness frees the warrior's power from habitual power sinks and lets him apply himself fully to the moment at hand. This position, summed up best by Socrates, is "It is better to make a mistake with the full force of your being than to carefully avoid mistakes with a trembling spirit."[16]

Castaneda

Carlos Castaneda seemed to spend much of his time with don Juan in an unrelenting state of fear and terror; yet he persevered on his path. He found ways to come to terms with the fear. Often, he relied on the presence or guidance of don Juan. He performed rituals and employed skills he learned from don Juan as ways of coping. Fear was a major obstacle and one of the major motivations in his journey.

Don Juan's philosophy about fear was simple—"In spite of fear one had to proceed with the course of one's acts."[17] He knew that warriors face, accept, and evaluate their fear—and then move beyond it. At times he used Carlos' fear as the main teaching tool of the moment. Most notably, he employed a technique he called *the worthy opponent.* He set Carlos against a powerful sorceress so that Carlos' only refuge was in what he was learning from don Juan. If he abandoned his path he could be annihilated at any moment. His fear, then, was his motivation for continuing his apprenticeship at that critical juncture. Fear, indeed, impels warriors to learn.

Later, in giving Carlos a detailed explanation of his training, don Juan offered his most cogent words on the topic of fear. "A warrior considers himself already dead so there is nothing for him to lose. The worst has already happened to him, therefore he's clear and calm."[18]

He repeated this theme in *The Fire from Within* by saying, "Warriors live with death at their side, and from the knowledge that death is with them they draw the courage to face anything . . . the worst that could happen to us is that we have to die, and since that is already our unalterable fate, we are free; those who have lost everything no longer have anything to fear."[19] And so in facing his fear, a warrior knows that ultimately he has nothing to lose. Therefore, he employs his training, uses his skills, and proceeds through the fear to continue on his path.

The Fourth Way

The Fourth Way sources referenced here seldom mention fear. Charles Tart offers a page of discussion about using low levels of fear, or intermittent occurrences of it, as motivation for personal growth work.[20] He offers an example of how to use fear to remind oneself to self-remember. He is explicit, as is Millman, in saying not to deny the fear, but to turn it into a positive action. After all, one does not want to give the fear more energy, which often occurs by denying it. Furthermore, engaging in a positive action after recognizing one's fearful state often diminishes the fear. The self-knowledge that comes from observing the fear experience and moving through it often dissolves the fear and brings long-term benefits.

I have used this process in therapy, sometimes taking a client to a cliff and teaching them to rappel down it. The physical metaphor illuminates the process of moving through fear by focusing on present actions. Picturing a future event, like lying crushed on the rocks below, paralyzes the person. Focusing on the precise actions in the moment permits them to get moving and succeed. It is a profound metaphor.

NLP

John Grinder, one of the founders of NLP, once employed the NLP modeling process with a remarkable Canadian actress named Viola Legere. He describes what he found in the book *Turtles All The Way Down*.[21] Viola Legere can make an impressive, passionate, total commitment to the character she is portraying, and Grinder wanted to know how she could become someone else so thoroughly and still maintain her sanity. He found that she is willing to enter what Grinder calls a *demon state,* in which she allows the actress part of herself to have free reign within the situation, without interference from ordinary consciousness. Now, this often happens to people who go insane. They cross a certain line, organize their identity states in a certain way, and cannot get back in touch with ordinary consciousness. In exploring how Viola Legere differed, Grinder discovered that she can engage in gloriously artistic madness and recover her normal self because she can set up what he called *contextual markers* that constrain the operation of the demon state to specific circumstances.

Viola Legere would not enter that demon state of commitment in her acting for Grinder unless he could satisfy her that the necessary contextual constraints were in place. This involved him functioning as her director, a person who would see to it that she knew when the performance was over and it was time to come back to her usual world. He also found that in acting it is important to have curtains and scripts that say "The End."

Grinder and others went on to use this model and other ideas to develop a workshop called "Prerequisites to Personal Genius." A primary prerequisite is to keep ordinary consciousness from interfering with the demon state. Fear can be a prime interference. When one is afraid, ordinary consciousness continually scans the environment for danger and interrupts the action with fear-based thoughts. With this distraction it is hard to let one's genius function effectively, because energy and focus are diverted from the arena of action. Grinder's ideas offer warriors ways of dealing with the fear to keep this from happening.

First, establish contextual markers that define when it is safe to engage in the demon state. This passionate, committed state involves a radical presence in the moment, calling for the maximum available energy to be focused on the action at hand. To make this commitment one must first establish the boundary conditions within which it is safe to do so. Beforehand, you should know when the demon state will begin, when it will end, and where it can occur. You need to establish *lifelines* to bring yourself back from the demon state. These could be another person who agrees to fulfil that function, an alarm clock, the sun going down, or other procedures that fit the circumstances. Once these constraints are in place, you can enter the demon state with total freedom to operate within those constraints. As strange as it sounds, the existence of constraints produces freedom.

There is another very important aspect of dealing with fear's potential disruption of these states of genius. We have learned from Gurdjieff that it is important not to lose oneself in identification. Self-remembering is the antidote to this, and Tart, as you recall from Chapter Six, characterizes self-remembering as a process involving setting aside some particular aspect of consciousness to keep track of one's totality. Grinder does it in a different way.

Many NLP techniques rely on the notion that an individual has any number of "parts" that control different functions, feelings, and beliefs. Grinder acknowledges, and the reader should keep in mind, that the term "parts" is just a way of speaking in shorthand about some complex neurological functions that lead us to occupy certain states of consciousness and personal organization. With that in mind, we can speak "as if" there are "parts" within us and we can construct some very useful techniques.

You can become aware of your present state and ask any of these relevant, usually unconscious, parts inside yourself to communicate with your conscious mind. You may receive a signal that could be a change in physical feeling in some part of your body, a voice, image, idea, or emotion. You can then use that signal to set up a dialogue between the part and your conscious self.

There are many applications of this process in NLP, but in terms of making it safe to enter the demon state, which is very much like (and often synonymous with) entering the unknown, you use the procedure to determine if a part of your unconscious is willing to monitor the world from a safety viewpoint. If something happens that you cannot handle within that particular demon state, the "safety part" will bring you back to ordinary consciousness if your safety requires it. As you set up this agreement within yourself, you must monitor your subjective experience very closely. You should ask not only if this agreement is acceptable to the "safety part," but if there are any other parts that object to this agreement. If there are, you recycle through the procedure of asking any objecting parts to communicate with your conscious self until you understand the objections. Then all involved parts must negotiate and construct an acceptable process of safety monitoring. Even so, you ask again if any of your parts object. NLP calls this "testing for ecology" and it is a crucial operation.

Once you have agreement that the "safety part" will take over the duty of monitoring the environment and will interrupt your demon state if your safety is threatened, you can enter the unknown with a one hundred percent, passionate commitment. In effect, you are your own lifeline. When you commit to action like this, and your survival is being well cared for in the background, fear is unlikely to induce your ordinary consciousness to interfere.

This does not mean you will never fear again. It means that you can acknowledge your fear, use it to help set up the appropriate constraints, and then have some part of you monitor the conditions of which you were fearful, without unnecessarily interfering with your commitment to action. Grinder's ideas are similar to, and in part inspired by, Castaneda. Grinder says, "One of the prerequisites for effective personal organization is an ability to make clean, one hundred percent commitments at each stage of whatever activities you engage in during the day. In Castaneda's metaphor this means being a warrior."[22]

NLP offers many methods to address emotions, but one of the more useful approaches for our present discussion is in the book *The Emotional Hostage*, by Leslie Cameron-Bandler and Michael Lebeau. They describe how many people feel like their emotions commandeer them, as if emotions had some life separate from the person who feels them. Indeed, it can feel that way if you have no way to take an active part in what emotions you experience. Then you feel powerless and the emotions seem to sweep in from some vague area outside your choice and awareness, leaving you a victim of their whims. Cameron-Bandler and Lebeau outline an elegant way in which people can become aware of the rich palette of emotions at their disposal, understand the value of each one, assess the usefulness of an emotion when they experience it, take whatever actions are indicated, and choose the emotional state that best supports those actions. Their approach uses many tools from the kit of NLP techniques, but we can outline enough of the steps to suit our current purposes.

Applying Cameron-Bandler and Lebeau's methods to the emotion of fear, we first employ our by-now-familiar sidekick, awareness. To keep emotions from taking us hostage, we must recognize our present emotional state. Of course, the more aware a person is, the sooner they recognize the onset of the emotion and the sooner they can respond appropriately.

Next, the warrior must understand the signal value, or as Cameron-Bandler and Lebeau call it, the functional attribute, of the emotion. They say:

> Your emotions are like a caring friend who is letting you know about a situation that you really need to respond to. Also, like a caring friend, your emotions may be letting you know about something that is unpleasant; they may even be giving you information in a way that's painful to hear. Nevertheless, it would be foolish to ignore what your emotional friend is trying to tell you.[23]

Every emotion, including fear, has some signal value for you. It is a message from your emotional center evaluating your circumstances or condition. This message is the function of the emotion. Cameron-Bandler and Lebeau list functional attributes for many emotions. For example, the functional attribute for regret is to tell you that you should have or could have done something differently than what you actually did. Guilt tells you that you transgressed a personal standard and warns you against doing it in the future. Anxiety signals you that there is something forthcoming for which you need to prepare better. We could go on for each feeling, and by determining the signal value, understand the positive function for each emotion. From this perspective all emotions, even the most painful, can be encountered with appreciation and respect. Instead of fighting the emotion, feeling victimized, or getting stuck there, you can use the signal value productively.

The third step is to generate curiosity and use it to evaluate the signal you have received, the circumstances you are in, and the outcomes you want. By doing so you will understand how this emotion fits into the context of your life and what you can do next to improve your condition.

Fourth, generate reassurance by recalling your past successes in dealing with similar circumstances. This is a way of mobilizing the resources you will need to act on the message from your emotions.

Next, vividly imagine yourself in the future responding to the current conditions, or others yet to come, in a productive and successful way. Use this procedure to generate feelings of confidence.

Cameron-Bandler and Lebeau call this process the "generative chain" of emotions. No matter what specific emotion you feel, the essential pattern is:

Triggering emotion → Respect/appreciation → Curiosity → Reassurance → Confidence.[24]

Applied specifically to fear, the warrior might use this generative chain process as follows:

1. Recognize the presence of fear and admit that you are feeling it.
2. With respect and appreciation for your emotional center's willingness to send you a message, determine the signal value. You will usually find that fear is a signal that you are in danger and that your body is preparing for flight or fight.
3. With a feeling of curiosity, determine the amount of risk that is present and whether you are willing to accept it. If not, you can leave the scene or find out what to do to reduce the danger to acceptable levels. Otherwise, accept the risk, check your lifelines, make sure your survival programs are operating in the background, and prepare for action.
4. Search through your past for resources that have enabled you to cope before with fearful situations. Perhaps you will find that you have strategies for escaping situations that are too dangerous, good judgment about risk taking, physical and mental capabilities to draw on, knowledge gleaned from previous

warriorship experiences, and—very important—that you know what to do when you don't know what to do.

5. If you are not already in the situation, vividly imagine yourself employing these resources and access confidence in your abilities. If you are already in the predicament, mobilize those resources as soon as possible and apply them confidently. If you are unable to do so, your best strategy may be to leave.

Accessing various emotions by choice, such as curiosity, acceptance, appreciation, and confidence, may seem like a difficult task when you are already afraid. However, there are many techniques for accessing and enhancing emotional states, several of which are in Chapter Seven of *The Emotional Hostage*.

We have explored many ideas about fear and approaches to dealing with it. There are some constants. All the warriorship teachers say that you must face your fear, evaluate it, and move beyond it. No one advises you to deny that the fear exists, and no one tells you to let fear hijack you and derail you from your course.

The methods advocated vary considerably, ranging from Trungpa's embracing of Basic Goodness, to Millman's nondramatization, through Cameron-Bandler and Lebeau's generative chain of emotional choice. The message, nevertheless, is clear: you cannot be a warrior and be a victim of your fear. You must continue to live strategically with awareness. You must learn the techniques for moving beyond fear. You must come to terms with fear so you can continue on your path with heart. Recall again Frank Herbert's "Litany Against Fear":

> I must not fear.
> Fear is the mind-killer.
> Fear is the little death that brings total obliteration.
> I will face my fear.
> I will permit it to pass over me and through me.
> And when it has gone past I will turn the inner eye to see its path.
> Where the fear has gone there will be nothing.
> Only I will remain.

Chapter Ten

Discipline

DISCIPLINE IS THE warrior's route to freedom and the path with heart and there is no warriorship without discipline. This sounds like bad news to those who investigate the warrior's way in search of freedom from routines and obligations of the ordinary world, but we will see that freedom is a product of discipline. In fact, the warrior seeks freedom through his discipline. The available forms of discipline are numerous, but in the warrior mythology they all have similar purposes and aims.

Warriorship, as we have seen, is no easy way of living. Its premises differ markedly from the ordinary, and the ordinary is not easy to leave behind. It has been ingrained since birth and is supported by the weight of society and its pervasive webs of reward and punishment. To take the path with heart, then, we must find a way of loosening our bonds with what has limited us. In so doing, we challenge our self-concepts, refocus our awareness, cut the tethers to our beliefs, rechannel our emotions, open to new sense perceptions, and find new filters through which to process information. This cannot be done in a hit-and-miss, "I'll get around to it when I feel like it" way. Warriorship requires discipline, and the warrior must exercise her discipline until the end of her life, or until she attains perfection. (Guess which one will come first!)

Fortunately, the act of discipline is also the act of living like a warrior. While you are practicing your discipline you are acting like a warrior, whether on a beginning or advanced level. Warriorship always occurs in the present, not in the future or past. When you act like a warrior in the moment, you are practicing your discipline and, in that moment, you are a warrior. Through discipline the warrior strives to live each non-ordinary moment as a warrior (remember, there are no ordinary moments) and tread with each step on her path with heart. If she does not, she wants to be aware of straying from the path as soon as possible so that she may choose again. But can we be more specific in our definition of discipline? Yes, on several levels.

Discipline *is* the process of awareness, of clearing away the clutter within, of weeding out the parasitic tensions, beliefs, and fears. It is a process of suspending judgment about whatever information awareness brings, so you can accept what you find in yourself, correct your course when you stray, and continue on your path. There are no moral condemnations. Your standards for evaluation are power, control, and integrity. Are you engaging in power leaks or applying power toward your quest? Are you in control of your faculties or being swept along by the push of external forces? Even if outer circumstances are horrible, are you in control of your inner aspects, such as focus and emotions? Are you acting with integrity so that you are not divided within yourself and so that you are congruent in action, thought, and feeling? There is no self-condemnation necessary if your performance doesn't measure up. Just be aware and choose again.

Discipline *is* the process of developing a true "I" and moving away from the fragmentation of identification. It allows you to follow the unbroken, unbent line of your intention and not be easily hijacked when other lines of force cross your path. It is the process of remembering yourself and developing your qualities harmoniously.

Discipline *is* learning how to match intention and action. It is perceiving that your actions match or mismatch your intentions. It is learning to apply your power so that your actions more truly manifest your intentions without wasting power in the process. It is attaining integrated functioning.

Discipline *is* learning to perceive basic goodness, and it is the effort you put forth to bring that kind of meditative awareness into action in life. It is what you do to learn to synchronize mind and body. It is looking for the Great Eastern Sun and looking away from the setting sun mentality.

Discipline *is* the struggle for impeccability. Through discipline you learn where your power leaks are and how you automatically invest power in unnecessary habits. Then, time after time, you plug the leaks and disrupt the routines. With progress, the leak does not stay open for as long and you choose where to apply your energy. You make your power more and more available for your warrior's quest. Finding that you still have power leaks does not mean you have failed as a warrior. Finding that you act automatically or habitually much of the time likewise is no cause for self-punishment. Being perfectly impeccable is not the standard that is required. Having impeccability as your intention, being aware of moments of non-impeccability, and making corrective choices is the warrior's daily task. That is her discipline.

Discipline *is* walking the path with heart. The substance of discipline is knowing your ultimate fate—that death will claim you, warrior or not—and continuing on your path anyway. As you become more disciplined you become aware more quickly when you have strayed from your path. You do not get so far off course as before, and you right yourself more quickly. Awareness of when you are and are not congruent with your path is the key, regardless of which particular practices you employ.

It is important to remember that discipline is not the outcome you attain. It is the daily actions, the practice, the putting-one-foot-in-front-of-the-other engaging in learning. If meditation is the form you choose, then meditation is your discipline. Enlightenment is not. You must find peace in the practice, letting it work its benefits in you, even if you do not know where it is getting you at the moment. Some days you will feel like you are getting somewhere, sometimes not. The effects of discipline are cumulative, adding up over the hours, days, and years of the warrior's life.

A feeling you must learn to accept is confusion and the sense that you are not getting "it," or that living like a warrior is just too complex and immense a task for you to attain. This is because it *is* such an immense and complex task, with endless levels of competence and seemingly infinite levels of subtlety to be mastered. When your skills improve, you become aware that there are levels you never had to deal with before. Each skill seems nested within others and you do not have to contend with higher or more subtle levels until you have attained a certain proficiency.

It is much like learning a new language and travelling to a foreign country. At first you feel overwhelmed as you try to communicate on the most basic level—ordering food, finding out where the bathrooms are, determining how much the taxi costs. When you are proficient at that level, you can start to feel overwhelmed with more complex communications—communicating in past or future tenses, having verbal exchanges that last more than two or three sentences, understanding detailed directions. Proficiency at this level allows you to feel overwhelmed by attempting conversations about the quality of life of the people there, understanding the political situation, explaining how things are in your country.

So too with warriorship discipline. Just when you feel like you are getting somewhere, your very proficiency brings you to the next level of complexity and you are just as challenged as before. Therefore, you cannot rely on the feeling of being overwhelmed or challenged as an accurate measure of progress. If you are becoming more capable, you will always be exposed to new challenges. You must analyze the circumstances and determine if you are being overwhelmed by the same order of difficulty as before, or if you are being overwhelmed by challenges of a different order. If the former is the case, you may be having difficulty on the particular step you are trying to learn. If the latter is true, you are continuing on your road to improvement.

This road to improvement is never-ending, and you should be suspicious of feelings of comfort with progress in your discipline. Does your comfort mean you are no longer exposing yourself to new levels of complexity and demand? Does it mean you are stagnating and avoiding challenges? Or does it mean that you accept the nature of progress and have found a peaceful way of dealing with the challenges you face? Remember, once you have crossed the frontier into the unknown you will be confused and not know what to do. These feelings occur for everyone, whether she crosses the frontier at her front door or on a night scuba dive in unknown waters. The difference is that the warrior knows what to do when she doesn't know what to do. The warrior embraces the confusion and recognizes the new challenge she faces in the unknown. You must realize that feeling challenged by your discipline can be one sign that you are engaging in it productively. You cannot expect to feel like you have mastered your discipline or that you have mastered warriorship. That status will always recede from you into the future, and your discipline is to act like a warrior in the present.

The Forms

There are innumerable forms of practice from which a warrior may pursue her discipline. Some are highly structured, some are not. Some have ancient roots, some are more modern. The particular form of discipline is probably less important than the commitment the warrior makes toward its practice. We have already outlined the purposes and directions of discipline, and as long as these are being met, the warrior should choose a form of discipline that fits her personal style and needs. This does not necessarily mean choosing the form that comes most easily. This could result in avoiding the very weaknesses you need to strengthen. On the other hand, choosing a form that doesn't fit you, just because it is difficult to do, does not mean you will get the most benefit. Analyze your strengths and weaknesses and look for a form that takes advantage of your strengths and helps you face your weaknesses. Remember, your weaknesses are usually good indicators of where to enter the unknown and where you need more knowledge. To avoid them leaves you forever vulnerable. At the same time, your discipline should be a source of renewal and joy, though a challenging one, and you should have confidence that it is a way of walking your path with heart.

Meditation

Trungpa describes the purposes and methods of meditation in the Shambhala tradition at length in his book. Jeremy Hayward elaborates on

Trungpa's teachings in *Perceiving Ordinary Magic.* The other principal exponent of meditation among our authors is Dan Millman, and his ideas are usually consistent with the Shambhala way.

Hayward defines two classes of meditation. The first he calls *trance type.* In this type of meditation one is trying to reach a different realm of experience than usual. Sometimes this realm is described as "higher" or more "inward." In this style of meditation one tries to close awareness of the senses and thoughts, turning inward to reach the other realm.

The other class of meditation is called *access type* and is favored by Hayward and Trungpa, although Hayward does allow for specific benefits of the trance type of meditation. Access type does not try to distinguish higher or other realms from the ordinary. The purpose is to train one's attention so that sensory impressions can be received more accurately and conceptions recognized in clearer detail. This will allow less filtering of sensory stimuli by habitual presuppositions which helps bring one to a clearer view of the genuine nature of oneself and one's surroundings. In the Shambhala view this means to make contact with basic goodness. Doing so helps to produce fearlessness, so access meditation is a tool for attaining fearlessness and genuineness. It is also a powerful way to synchronize mind and body, which should help to promote integration in one's functioning.

Hayward also refers to access-type meditation as mindfulness-awareness training, or at times, bare attention. Mindfulness-awareness training for a warrior takes place in two venues. The first is sitting meditation practice; the second is in action. Hayward offers the following description of the sitting meditation practice:

> It simply is a way to become attentive to our thoughts, emotions, perceptions, bodily sensations, and environment, so that who and what we are begin to be clearly and precisely seen. We sit in a relaxed and upright posture, with straight spine, open chest, hands resting naturally on the thighs. To take such a posture already expresses the genuine dignity of being human. To remain in that posture during the ups and downs of our thought and emotional processes expresses the fundamental confidence of trusting in unconditional goodness. The eyes are open with soft

gaze, slightly down, and we take the same attitude to the other senses—open but not fixed or harshly striving to experience something. As we sit there, we allow our minds to identify with the outgoing breath, to go out with it, and then to return to be attentive to the posture as the breath comes in. As thoughts, feelings, and physical sensations begin to pop up, we note them and let them be as they are, not trying to push them away, or holding onto them and indulging them. We begin to become mindful of the precise details of our thought and perceptual processes and also aware of the relationship between them. A thought or feeling arises, and then it goes away. Where it arises from and whence it goes, who can say? But occasionally we might catch a glimpse of non-thought, of open mind. A glimpse can be tremendously refreshing. It is such a relief to realize that we can afford to let go of our conceptualizing process altogether. Such a glimpse of our basic nature of unconditioned goodness brings with it a sense of gentleness and tenderness toward ourselves.[1]

Hayward goes on to say that this type of meditation helps us see how we are limited by prejudices and conditioning, whether imposed by ourselves or others. Once we are familiar with our conditioning, we can find gaps in it where the unconditioned might shine through and we can apprehend it directly.

This is similar to Castaneda's training in *stopping the world*. Through his discipline Carlos sought to escape from his internal dialogue long enough to elude his usual description of the world. Then other possibilities could emerge from the unknown and other perceptions could become possible, even finding non-ordinary realities. By stopping the world Castaneda could perceive the world and its beings more directly in terms of lines of energy or emanations. Castaneda may have been writing this metaphorically. Still, the point is that through a discipline that diminishes the effects of the usual world descriptions we employ, that lessens the effects of our usual filters on perception and alters our habitual ways of seeing things, we arrive at the ability to perceive different levels of reality. We can speak of it as Trungpa's basic goodness, don Juan's bands of emanations, or the physicist's enfolded order. We arrive at other levels of reality by changing beliefs and perceptual style. We do that by overcoming habits.

Notice that this type of meditation requires no particular religious beliefs in celestial realms, personages, or entities. This is consistent with Trungpa's term "secular enlightenment," which is the goal of Shambhala warriorship.

The other venue for meditation in the warrior's way is action, where the warrior goes beyond sitting practice and engages the world in a broader sense. As Socrates said to Dan Millman, "Meditation is the action of inaction; yet you are quite correct that the warrior's way is more dynamic. Ultimately, you will learn to meditate your every action."[2] This is a process of bringing mindfulness-awareness training into motion and expressing its vitality. Millman, while he coached college gymnastics, taught his athletes to meditate. They did this not only as sitting practice, but with the goal of meditating every action during a performance. Think of the quality of action that would flow from being in a state free of distractions, either internal or external, where all that you were doing in the moment was the action at hand. This is similar to John Grinder's notion of *demon states* described in Chapter Nine.

Hayward says, "Mindfulness is when mind is fully present with whatever action we are executing."[3] He goes on to describe how every action is complete, with a beginning, a middle, and an end. Being involved in the completeness of every action, whether writing a letter, shaking hands, making love, sleeping, or painting, you will attain a sense of appreciation for the present moment as important and magnificent in itself. One action is not just a springboard to the next thing on your agenda but is significant in its own right. "Such appreciation of the present moment," writes Hayward, "is known as 'nowness'—the realization that, at each moment, this very moment is the only occasion of your life, uncorrupted by past or future."[4] Mindfulness-awareness training, at its ultimate, brings one to a state where each moment can be lived with full application of one's personal power.

Hayward and Trungpa believe that other discipline forms often make a valuable bridge between sitting practice and action in everyday life. Let us now explore some other forms of discipline that a warrior might choose.

Art Forms

For centuries, forms of discipline have developed in the Orient as ways to train the mind, condition and train the body, and synchronize both. They contain the essential elements of mindfulness-awareness training in the realm of action. Here a warrior can find many choices that suit her particular needs—from small movements emphasizing precision of expression to large, fast, powerful movements requiring accurate blending of skill and strength. Trungpa himself practiced the Japanese art of *ikebana,* or flower arranging. In this and other Japanese art forms, the artist uses her discipline to train the mind-heart to be open to the harmony that underlies all of nature and uses herself as the instrument to express that harmony. Hayward says that the flower arrangement itself "is a reflection of the student's state of mind, of how tight or relaxed, how scattered or attentive, how embarrassed or confident, how confused or balanced, he or she felt as each particular flower was placed."[5] A teacher of ikebana, Trungpa said, "Ikebana discipline is not just arranging pretty flowers, making them into a beautiful arrangement. More fundamentally, it is a reflection of oneself."[6] Many Oriental art forms share this quality of the person becoming a bridge of expression between the underlying harmony and elegance of nature and the relative state of her body/mind. Other forms include *kyudo* (archery), *chanoyu* (tea ceremony), and *calligraphy.*

This ability to bridge between the artist and the underlying nature that produces both the artist and the art is not limited to Oriental forms. Indeed, any artistic endeavor has this capacity. Painting, writing, sculpture, composing, and the like can all produce the experience of self-expression flowing from the artist's grounding in underlying nature. Practicing art can engage one's demon state and result in the experience of "nowness" produced by mindfulness-awareness training. This is true also for the performing arts like dancing, acting and, music. There is the opportunity for the artist to engage so completely in the nowness of the moment that her expression can be as pure as anything in the Oriental arts traditions. Do not think, however, that all artists are warriors. Art forms can be used as warriorship disciplines when the artist uses her discipline to train herself in impeccability, seek the unknown in the warrior's way, and walk the path with heart. One can be a very successful and talented artist and still not be a warrior.

The same can be said for the martial arts. Warriorship is often equated in common usage with fighting, and it is tempting to think of martial artists as warriors. Actually, martial arts can be marvelous warriorship disciplines, but simply engaging in martial arts will not make one a warrior. You can become an athlete, a fighter, or a soldier and not be a warrior in the sense that we have been using the term. The practice of warriorship transcends the particular discipline, and those who choose the martial arts path can easily be seduced by the "martial" rather than the "artistic" aspects. Behind most schools of martial arts, particularly Oriental ones, there is a rich tradition of philosophy and ethics. There is often a component of sitting meditation or an active seeking of balance and blending with the forces of one's own intentions, movements, and awareness, the same factors of one's opponent, and the underlying relationship to nature. Being mindful of oneself, the martial artist senses how her movements are expressions of her inner state in relation to the world. This type of warrior knows that victory in fighting is not determined by effort, but by how clearly she carries her inner state into action. Given comparable levels of skill, the martial artist whose technique expresses mindfulness and a harmonious relationship to the world around her will carry the day over one who is less mindful and less in balance with the world.

Somatic Forms

Martial and performing arts are somatic in that they involve movement in space, and movement itself is the artistic product, rather than a portrait, statue, or symphony. These arts are also somatic in that they fuse mind and body in a synchronized expression of movement. There are other practices that focus on the unity of mind and body where increased awareness is the intended goal. There is not a specific product, such as increased proficiency in a martial arts technique, or a performance such as a concert or play. The warrior practices the somatic form as a direct means of enhancing awareness, and one could argue that these are types of meditation practice. Of course, it depends on how the somatic form is used. You could engage it with a warrior's perspective and focus, or go through the physical actions with a wandering mind. One way will work as a warriorship discipline, the other will be a nice way to kill time.

There is both variety and similarity in the various somatic forms. Some focus on quality of movement, some on breathing, some on posture, some on providing certain kinds of stimulation. Nevertheless, they all promote higher levels of awareness, focus of attention, improved functional abilities, and advancement of integration between the parts of oneself and between the self and the environment. Along the way, people who engage in these forms usually develop a sense of well being and find that they can live with greater comfort and ease. Health problems tend to get better and, as with all true disciplines, a sense of grounding and direction emerges.

Since activities with such varying foci produce similar results, there must be some underlying theme that unites them. In a book called *The Body of Life,* the late Feldenkrais Practitioner Thomas Hanna proposed a theory of what he calls the *archesoma.*[7] This theory stems from the view that all life has evolved under a particular set of circumstances requiring movement for survival. Organisms whose movement is efficient for successful adaptation survive and reproduce. Therefore, each species has a functional core, the archesoma, that is a basic system of movements in the three dimensions of space and the dimension of time. This system of movements must be efficient and must blend with the environment if a species and its individual members are to survive. The archesoma is more than physical. It is the enabling core of life itself and is therefore the basis of all functioning—acting, sensing, thinking, and feeling. There is a phylogenetic, or species-wide, archesoma and there is an ontogenetic, or individual, archesoma as well. The phylogenetic archesoma draws the blueprint for adaptation and survival, but things can go awry for individuals depending on their experience and learning.

The state of one's archesoma is detectable. External observers can identify its condition by its pattern of movements. The individual observes by sensing proprioceptive feedback directly—in other words, through awareness. If there are distortions in the archesoma, there will be distortions in specific functions of that individual. There is no room here for the division of the person into "body" and "mind." Archesomatic distortion affects the entire being and compromises one's relationship with the environment. For human beings, some amount of archesomatic distortion is almost inevitable, either because of specific trauma or faulty learning encouraged by "civilization." But our distortion does not have to be permanent.

The somatic forms address these distortions through the medium of awareness. With awareness, the innate systems of self-correction are mobilized and the archesoma itself improves. There are many ways to promote this awareness.

Feldenkrais

The Feldenkrais Method of Awareness Through Movement was described in Chapter Four. The results sometime seem magical, and beginners are likely to attribute their improvement to the specific movements involved. They often think that one does a particular movement for the neck, another for the back, and so on. The "magic," though, is not in the movements, but in the quality of attention and the explorations of nonhabitual patterns that were never learned or have been forgotten in the individual archesoma. Thus, the learning goes well beyond a particular movement to the improvement of functioning in general. Recall that from the archesoma all functions emerge. Therefore, one lays the foundation for greater proficiency in all aspects.

Awareness Through Movement can be done alone or in groups. In many areas of North and South America, Europe, and Australia there are classes and workshops in this method. There are also books and audiotapes available for private study. Besides doing the actual Awareness Through Movement lessons, this approach has application in real-life circumstances. The model of how to learn new skills through increased awareness of habitual patterns and safe exploration of nonhabitual possibilities can be applied to any functional limitation. Indeed, the mix of structured lessons and real-world application is a potent discipline.

Individual Feldenkrais lessons, known as Functional Integration®, can be obtained from practitioners certified by the Feldenkrais Guild.

In these sessions learning is communicated through the physical guidance of the practitioner, who establishes a special linkage with the student through touch—as if two nervous systems are combined. The practitioner augments the student's awareness and intentions with her own, leading to learning that is tailor-made for that student. Receiving learning at the hands of someone else is not likely to become a discipline. However, Functional Integration lessons can open doors that have seemed shut forever and can propel the student in the direction of a disciplined use of the processes of awareness and exploration.

The most potent way to engage the Feldenkrais Method is to take the training to become a practitioner. This is in large part a warriorship training. Learning "what to do when you don't know what to do," embracing the unknown and the feelings of confusion that come with it, relying on internal reference points, expanding awareness, and not-doing habitual activities are all learned in the training. These skills are needed to practice the method effectively and the practitioner engages in her discipline with every lesson she teaches.

Yoga

Yoga is one of the world's oldest somatic disciplines. Often called the eightfold path, it goes far beyond the scope of physical exercise. The premises of Hatha yoga are rooted in a metaphysical philosophy that encompasses body, mind, and soul, considered to be the three components that make up human beings. Attending to these factors produces a person who is detached from the vagaries of worldly existence and lives with equanimity and harmony. Silva, Mira, and Shyam Mehta have written a beautifully illustrated book called *Yoga the Iyengar Way.* In it they say there are three needs to be satisfied if one is to live a contented life. "The physical need is health; the psychological need is knowledge; and the spiritual need is inner peace," write the Mehtas.[8]

The goals of yoga are ultimately different from warriorship. Gurdjieff, remember, developed his work as "The Fourth Way" to distinguish it from the way of the fakir, the way of the monk, and the way of the yogi. He viewed the first three ways as proven paths to knowledge and harmonious development, but all three require a withdrawal from the world that Gurdjieff sought to bypass. Nevertheless, the discipline of yoga can be an excellent way to plug power leaks, develop detachment from outcomes, control internal dialogue, and produce an expanded relationship with the universe. The practice of yoga can be an excellent discipline form for warriors to develop inner harmony and synchronization of body, mind, and spirit.

Āsanas are the physical poses of yoga and are probably the part of yoga most familiar to Westerners. The poses are psychophysical in nature. Going beyond physical exercise, they form the basis for a kind of meditation in movement. As with the Feldenkrais Method, keen attention to what you are doing is essential. Awareness is heightened and spread throughout the body, not concentrated on a single part. Yet, the quality of attention to any specific area is maintained. The whole self receives high-quality attention as part of the total picture. The Mehtas describe the process like this: "In order to keep the knee straight, attention is focused on the knee. This is concentration. Then, holding the attention there, the mind moves on to the next focus and from there to another, until attention is diffused all over the body without any lessening of intensity. *This is meditation.*"[9] This is also an example of the kind of inclusive attention advocated by Feldenkrais and Tart as discussed in Chapter Six.

The Sanskrit word *ātman* refers to the soul, or inner self, of all beings. When āsanas are practiced properly, the ātman rises to the surface and expresses itself. Doing the yoga poses, then, is also a way to contact and express one's essence. Of course, the poses must be correctly practiced, both in terms of moving into the positions and in terms of the right frame of mind. To become ego-involved in achieving success, to compete with others or oneself, or to otherwise be attached to specific outcomes can result in expression of the ego rather than the ātman. For this reason, yoga is usually best learned from a teacher who is sensitive to the physical, psychological, and spiritual needs of her students.

Besides the āsanas, yoga has specific disciplines for controlling the breath and drawing the senses inward, away from external focus. These processes are best undertaken after some competence with the āsanas is attained. Mastering the breath and stilling the senses achieve control of the mind. Like well-executed āsanas, breath mastery and sensory stillness are forms of somatic meditation. They lead to a sense of stillness, a state of equanimity, in which one "is freed from the twin compulsions of fear and desire."[10]

There are even more advanced forms of yoga meditation that lead to the revelation of one's true self in pure form and to a state called *Samādhi,* which is, according to the Mehtas, "a transcendent state beyond meditation, where the psychological process stops. Consciousness becomes totally absorbed in the soul. A state of truth and bliss."[11] This reveals the ultimate goal of yoga, which is a joining of the individual soul and the universal soul. To quote the Mehtas again, "Yoga deals with the most profound of mysteries, the essential nature of the human being in relation to the universe."[12]

In Castaneda's system, living like a warrior was not the end of the path. Carlos was led by don Juan to become a *man of knowledge,* and the warrior's life was a prerequisite. Yoga is similar. The discipline of yoga practice leads to what we have called impeccability. With this level of personal power we can approach the source of knowledge itself. In yoga this is a highly spiritual state, requiring no adherence to any particular religion, in which the individual being is united with the transcendent, universal principle that is the source of all things.

Eutony, Alexander, and Other Somatic Forms

There are more somatic forms than we have space to address here, but we can refer to a few more. In Europe, and to a lesser degree in other parts of the world, *Eutony* is a powerful and respected somatic practice. Founded by a remarkable woman named Gerda Alexander, Eutony is taught in nearly every major university in Western Europe in the areas of music, theater and, physical education. In Denmark, home of the Eutony school, Eutony is also taught in primary schools, expectant mother programs, psychotherapy schools, and institutions for the retarded. In 1983 Feldenkrais practitioner David Bersin interviewed Gerda Alexander, and the interview was published in *Somatics.* Bersin wrote in the prelude to the article, "Eutony consists of a system of training designed to teach improved perceptual and motor control of posture and movement in everyday life and in the treatment of patients with neuro-muscular disorders."[13]

Alexander explains that the word Eutony derives from the Greek *eu* meaning good or harmonious, and the Latin *tonus* meaning tension. Therefore, Eutony means well-balanced tension. Alexander sees the control and proper application of tension throughout one's body as the vehicle not only for action, but for associated emotional states, contact with the environment, and artistic creativity and expression. In Eutony students are taught what they call *presence,* which consists of "awareness of mind, sensation of the outer form of the body, in contact with the surroundings, awareness of breathing, circulation, tissues, inner space with organs and bones."[14] Far from withdrawing attention from some subjects, Eutony seeks to expand it. Students are invited to move with presence and awareness, releasing contractions and parasitic synergies while observing their inner space (muscles, bone structures, circulation, sensation of carriage of the body), breathing, and attending to the environment. Alexander sees this kind of experience as connected to spirit, not separate from it. She says, "What I want is to make it possible for everybody to experience the reality of the spiritual part in themselves here and now, included in our body, in connection with the spiritual part of the universe . . . consciousness about our body in all details as a manifestation of spiritual connection."[15] This idea is akin to yoga, in which body, mind, and spirit are part of a unified whole and seeing them as such brings health, synchronization, and harmony.

Another Alexander, F. Matthias Alexander, who preceded Gerda Alexander and is no relation to her, developed his own respected somatic form. *The Alexander Technique* derived from his problems as a Shakespearean actor in Australia. Plagued by a tendency to lose his voice and getting no lasting help from medicine, Alexander set out to decipher the problem by observing himself in a set of mirrors. He discovered that he distorted his throat by making a subtle motion of moving his head back and down. This involved tightening the muscles in the back of the neck and elevating the chin. He did this habitually, not only when he was going to recite, but whenever he began any activity. Alexander found a way to teach himself to begin actions with an almost imperceptible motion of moving the head up and letting the body follow, which formed the basis of self-correction. In studying others he determined that the faulty movement of the head often precedes and triggers other damaging habitual responses, contracting the spine hundreds of times a day and leading to a generally poor use of oneself.

Alexander developed his ideas into a technique that has had wide application for people involved in all walks of life, from theater to science to philosophy. George Bernard Shaw praised Alexander's work, as did John Dewey and Aldous Huxley. In accepting the Nobel Prize in 1973, ethologist Niko Tinbergen spoke at length about the Alexander Technique and its potential to benefit people in terms of performance and in dealing with stress-related ailments.

Like many other somatic pioneers, Alexander recognized the importance of how people use themselves and how this use can be degraded and distorted through faulty habits. He recognized the power of awareness in learning to overcome problems and to advance along one's path.

The works of some of the other pioneers are available to the public these days. Milton Trager has developed *The Trager Method*, an awareness-based system of working with people both with the hands and with movements known as Mentastics. Charlotte Selver and Charles Brooks teach a system based on the findings of somatic innovator Elsa Gindler, called *Sensory Awareness*. Anglo-American philosopher Alan Watts, after learning of Sensory Awareness, was moved to exclaim, "Why, this is the living Zen!"

The core of the somatic forms involves awareness and learning to improve functioning. They dismiss the common cultural notion that body and mind are divided, stressing the necessity for a holistic approach. These forms are available as part of the personal discipline of modern warriors. One needs to remember, though, that the form is not a place for attachment. It is a vehicle for training awareness, overcoming habits, learning attention, and synchronizing body, mind, and spirit. It is a way to help develop impeccability. There is no sense in deciding one form is right or wrong compared to others. Each warrior selects the discipline that works best for her and realizes that for someone else other forms work just as well. In the Appendix is a list of resources for finding teachers or other information about the various somatic forms discussed in this chapter.

Gurdjieff Practices

Discipline and practice are hallmarks of The Fourth Way. Although one can appreciate this work for its cosmology and approach it as a comprehensive system of psychology, actually doing the work is a fundamental requirement for real progress.

Self-observation is a major practice in the Gurdjieff work. The idea is to learn all you can about yourself, both in general and specific situations. It involves observing more than the intellectual process; it includes our emotions, body, and intuitions as well. Self-observation trains the attention and opens up new knowledge about ourselves and the world. It is a prerequisite to awakening from the consensus trance.

Done well, though, self-observation must be an honest attempt to learn the truth about yourself and how you function, rather than to search for ways in which you meet your preconceived expectations, or to find justification for criticizing yourself for falling short of your ideals. It is a practice for attending to *everything* in an open-minded way without filtering attention through *a priori* beliefs about the way things should be. Find out what is! Even the most ordinary things, feelings, or thoughts can be surprisingly rich with information if you observe openly and honestly. It is always tempting to look at a practice that sounds simple, like self-observation, and think that you are already skilled at it. Though we all have a certain level of skill, there is much more to it than what usually passes for knowing oneself. Do it deliberately, in a focused way, as a disciplined act, and the reality in which you live and the way you relate to yourself will change.

Another awareness-based practice in The Fourth Way is self-remembering. As you may recall from our earlier exploration, this is a disciplined method for overcoming the fragmenting effects of identification, integrating our faculties under conscious control, and awakening from the machine-like life known as consensus trance. There are several ways of practicing self-remembering, but they have in common the process of assigning one part of consciousness to be aware of how the other parts function. This helps to lead us closer to realizing our *self*, the true captain of the ship, rather than to let a successive parade of individual parts masquerade as the leader. It is a means of drawing closer to the true "I." In *Waking Up*, Charles Tart provides not only a discussion of self-remembering and the difficulty of describing it in words, but offers a guide to one form of practice. The reader would be well advised to read that section of his book entitled "Practices," and if interested in pursuing Fourth Way disciplines further, to consult his extensive bibliography.

The Gurdjieff work is a complete system for pursuing impeccability. Promoting the harmonious development of human beings, it offers cognitive, emotional, and motion-oriented forms of discipline practices. Gurdjieff at times called himself a teacher of temple dances, referring to systems of movement and expression he encountered on his search for knowledge. You can find more information about these forms in *Meetings with Remarkable Men*, both the book and Peter Brook's movie by the same name. Students of the Fourth Way participate in activities ranging from listening to music in special ways to physical labor, all with the idea of promoting their development along designated lines.

Following the numerous Fourth Way disciplines can be difficult to do on one's own, especially if you seek a comprehensive approach to this work. The help of a Gurdjieff group is often needed. Again, Tart should be consulted for ways of evaluating whether this is a good idea for any specific individual and for advice on how to select a group. Gurdjieff himself maintained that a teacher is necessary for truly awakening, and though others would argue with him about the necessity, it can be a great help.

Control and Freedom

Development of impeccability is a major reason to engage in a warrior discipline. This means the warrior will gain more and more control over herself. This means she can live strategically, having not only clear intentions, but the ability to actualize those intentions. It means the warrior can enter the unknown and not fall apart. It means that the flow of events does not derail the warrior from her strategy, nor does the power of her former habits.

There are probably no areas of human functioning that cannot be brought under a substantial degree of control. There are many techniques for controlling cognitions, others for controlling emotions, and others for controlling movements. Even instinctive functions can be brought under volitional control through such practices as yoga and biofeedback. Such control is not developed out of fear of the functions, but to plug energy leaks and to enhance the capacity for response and functioning in all centers. When the warrior needs to respond to a situation, she must have her capacities available for use. Her senses will detect stimuli, her thoughts and decisions will be clear, her emotions will energize her decisions, and her body will act effectively. This is control and it does not come easily.

Controlling external events and other people is another matter. Being effective in action and sensing the pattern of occurrences around her, the warrior can influence what happens to her. Still, what occurs outside is not certain. So the warrior, according to don Juan, calculates everything. She exercises self-control. But there comes a time to abandon control. There is a time for action outside the form of one's discipline. In martial arts it is often said that you will not use what you practice when actually fighting. This is the other side of discipline—letting go.

Letting go, according to Trungpa, is relaxing within discipline. For don Juan, after the warrior has completed her calculations, she acts. She acts with abandon, with the full force of her being. Letting go within discipline, releasing the form of the discipline to use the abilities cultivated by it, taking the plunge you have prepared for, is also part of the warrior's discipline. Make no mistake. This is no excuse to avoid discipline and act recklessly. As Trungpa says, "Letting go is living in the challenge. But this does not mean living with a constant crisis."[16] The warrior's discipline gives her the tools she needs to grasp her cubic centimeter of chance, but letting go is when she actually does it. No matter how skilled you become in practice of your discipline form, you must acquire the judgment and ability to let go at the right time. Shivas Irons said in *Golf in the Kingdom*, "All skill involves a certain measure of spontaneity and unconscious functioning: no one can create beauty, be it in a work of art or on a golfing links, unless he has both disciplined control and the ability to let go to the sudden glimmer."[17]

So, discipline and letting go lead to freedom for the warrior. From the practice of her discipline she becomes more impeccable. She also becomes more skilled and more in control of herself, leading to effective action in the world. From this platform she can dive into action, at times finding capabilities she did not know she had. This is great freedom—freedom from former limitations, freedom from being blown like a leaf by external forces, freedom from the paralyzing power of fear. It is also freedom to act toward something, to respond with power to circumstances, to take one's destiny in one's own hands. It is the freedom to walk the path with heart.

Chapter Eleven

Magic, Will and Detachment

THE WARRIOR'S DISCIPLINE gives him skills and allows him to develop his being. This is essential in acquiring impeccability. His discipline also leads the warrior into the realm of magic but this is not the magic of the illusionist on stage, nor of the witchcraft of the Middle Ages. Castaneda used the term "sorcery" in his early books to describe the unbelievable things that don Juan and don Genaro could do. Later he used the term *nagual* to indicate that they had access to a non-ordinary realm in which there were possibilities that were inexplicable from a state of ordinary awareness. The warrior's magic, then, must be thought of in a different way than most people use the term.

Magic is not a property of events or substances. It is an attribute that we make in our minds when we observe something that does not fit into our current scheme of reality. We do not always deem something magical when it does not fit; more often, we deny its existence or simply do not see it. However, when something occurs that is inexplicable by our current reality framework, and we cannot send it away by denial, we often say it is magical. So, magic is dependent on our reference points and power of explanation. When we cannot describe how something works, if it's outside our frame of reference, we attribute it to magic.

Warriors learn to enjoy magic because they have flexible frames of reference and are good at suspending or shifting world descriptions. When an event does not fit into the current map of reality, warriors realize that they need to update their map or shift to another one. They do not demand that the phenomenon fit into their current map as is. They can accept its existence without demanding an explanation from a particular reality framework, especially the framework of consensus trance. New data is used to enhance the warrior's view of reality. From the position of consensus trance, the view of reality is used to validate or invalidate new data. No such judgment is necessary when one has a flexible map of reality. Things are neither "real" nor "unreal." They either fit a given map or they don't. They belong to the current reality program or they belong to another one. It is not a question of real or unreal, valid or false, ordinary or magical.

This was the great difficulty Castaneda had in his apprenticeship. Don Juan continually created situations where things happened that did not fit Carlos' fixed view of reality. After a particular "hallucinogenic" experience—say where Carlos had experienced himself as a crow flying through the air—he would pester don Juan afterward with questions like "Did I *really* fly?" Don Juan's whole point was that the word "really" is inoperative. There are separate realities and he was trying to teach Carlos to travel among them. Stubbornly, Carlos insisted on labeling the experiences hallucinations, unreal, or magical. To view them as valid phenomena would be tantamount to admitting that his scheme of reality was not the true reality, and for years that was too frightening to allow. Later, Carlos learned that the only way to cope with his experiences was to suspend his judgments of what was allowable within a certain defined reality and to deal with the event directly. This allowed him to function in the worlds of alternate realities.

With this willingness to accept that one's subjective reality is not the only possibility, warriors can appear to create magic or have magic powers. But, this is just a matter of point of view. Nothing magical is happening at all. Events are consistent within a particular map of reality. However, to an observer who witnesses those same events and tries to fit them into a different map, the events will seem like magic. A better word, though, would be otherworldly; but to use it is to admit that there are other worlds and that is too threatening for many people to contemplate. Hence, they reject the experience, bend their perception of it to fit their reality, or resort to the explanation of magic, which is no explanation at all.

The bottom line here is that the map is not the territory. From the Castaneda point of view, it is not necessary to assume that there is a territory. There may be, but the warrior knows that his perceptions probably will never lead him to it. They will, though, allow him to shift among innumerable possible maps of reality. These other maps are in the realm of the unknown, and it is his quest to seek the unknown and acquaint himself with a diverse selection of alternate realities. As we found in Chapter Seven, a world is created by an act of perception, when one reality is formed from all the mathematically possible realities. Such is the nature of perception. Our life experiences and our belief systems tend to limit the types of perceptions we can make. This is a limitation with which the warrior struggles all his life. His task is to increase his experience base and to shed the straitjacket of fossilized beliefs, so he becomes fluid and flexible in what he can perceive and experience.

Ordinary Magic

Another view of the topic of magic is that magic is not otherworldly at all, but is produced by a "cleaner" act of perception that allows the person to apprehend a phenomenon of the regular world that was there all along.

This often happens accidentally to us when we notice something that we had not noticed before in a familiar situation. Listening to a familiar piece of music we suddenly hear the viola that we never heard before. We see a detail or a color in a painting that we never saw in a dozen prior viewings. By misapplying cause and effect reasoning we could call this magic, but we really have superstition. What happens is that we link the appearance of the new detail with some event or action that just preceded it and suddenly we have made a new superstition. This is sometimes called magical thinking, but the term "magic" is used in a way far removed from how we are using it here.

In true cause and effect reasoning one must specify the cause, determine that it produces the effect, and specify the rules of transformation involved. When we leave out this last step we have engaged in superstitious thinking and have left the realm of the very type of logic to which we appeal. We have stated that through some mysterious transformation the cause has produced the effect. Since we do not know how this was done, it does not fit with our explanation of reality and we attribute it to magic. Superstition is a more accurate word, though.

The kind of magic we are talking about now derives from a shift in mindfulness that warriors seek. This mindfulness is a product of impeccability, discipline, and of a release of rigid beliefs about what is possible. This is along the lines of thought proposed by Hayward and Trungpa, hence Hayward's choice of *Perceiving Ordinary Magic* as the title of his book. This kind of magic does not involve unnatural powers of the warrior over the phenomenal world. We have already heard from several sources that such powers or special abilities are by-products of the warrior's skill and discipline. Should the warrior get attached to them he will be stalled in his quest and miss the point of warriorship entirely.

In Hayward's point of view everything contains magic, but we often lack the ability to see it. As we become more mindful and awaken from habitual manners and outlooks we can connect with that magical, yet ordinary, ground that gives rise to things and events. Trungpa says that this *super-perception* requires a relaxing of the mind that allows you to get your personal interpretations out of the way so you can discern the principle of magic that is in everything. This is another way of saying that when you *stop the world* magic happens. Of this kind of perception Hayward says, "Such transformed perception could be called 'ordinary magic.' It is ordinary because it is hidden from us by nothing other than our reluctance to see it, by habitual beliefs in struggle, separateness and fear."[1] Again we find that interpretations and beliefs are the barriers that deny access to the magical realm of greater ability, perception, and knowledge.

Trungpa and Hayward speak of a reality that lies beyond the province of belief. Through the discipline of meditation the warrior learns to contact the basic reality that is unrelated to belief or thought.

It is what was there before the intellect imposed interpretations and judgments. It is primordial reality. Trungpa says to find this reality you must relax your mind into it, and this means you must learn to find nowness through meditation. By entering the present completely, you approach things without bias and you are neither for nor against things. Neither are they for nor against you.

Trungpa speaks of relaxing to a cloud by simply looking at it, or relaxing to a raindrop and experiencing its genuineness. This ability allows the warrior unlimited perception. Consciousness, sensing, and the objects of perception blend into the act of perceiving and you can have not only sight, but super-sight; not only hearing, but super-hearing; and so on for all the senses. The term super-natural takes on new meaning. Pure perception, unbiased by our conditioning, leads to the super-natural. This is magic to Trungpa. Magic is invoked when the magic inherent in all things is accessible. As he wrote in *Shambhala*, "You might think that something extraordinary will happen to you when you discover magic. Something extra-ordinary does happen. You simply find yourself in the realm of utter reality, complete and thorough reality."[2]

You cannot invoke magic by aggression or with violent intent. Finding a gentle state of being in yourself is essential, because if you have conflict in you, you cannot find the magic abiding beyond conflict. The Shambhala warrior has trained himself in gentleness and openness, the prerequisites for invoking magic. Without conflict and without shields, the warrior enters the state of openness that lies beyond aggression. It is his fundamental act of bravery.

In the Shambhala model, magic relates to a principle called *drala*. Literally translated, it means *beyond the enemy*, which means it lies beyond the dualities of good and evil, right and wrong, or friend and foe. It is thus free of conflict and, therefore, beyond the enemy. Drala is a kind of energy that can descend on the warrior when he invokes magic. It is a power that can release the warrior from any kind of problem or hesitation, free him from whatever arises in his state of mind. This energy is strength. It puts the warrior in touch with the basic goodness of himself and the world around him. For such a warrior, discipline and delight are united.

Besides laying the foundation through sitting meditation, Trungpa gives three specific ways to invoke drala:

1. Invoking *external drala.* This is the process of invoking magic in the physical environment. It is a way of promoting one's warriorship discipline by how one relates to the surroundings. Through awareness and attention to detail the warrior creates harmony around him. The warrior wants his environment to reflect his essential attributes. "When you express gentleness and precision in your environment, then real brilliance and power can descend,"[3] advises Trungpa. For external drala to descend the warrior must express an attitude of sacredness toward the physical environment.

2. Invoking *internal drala.* The warrior also evokes drala in his body through the way he relates to it. Besides regarding his body as one basically good human body, the warrior attends to how he dresses, cleans, nurtures, and maintains it. He makes a proper relationship to food and how he uses his mouth in general. Treating his body according to its basic goodness sets the stage for internal drala to come as the warrior synchronizes his body with the phenomenal world.

3. Invoking *secret drala.* When the warrior invokes the principles of both external and interna drala, the product is secret drala. Trungpa says "you provoke tremendous wakefulness, tremendous nowness . . . a feeling of being powerfully in the present."[4] In this state the warrior's life is energetic and delightful. He experiences neither problems nor hesitation, and a marvelous wind of power is available to him.

In the sense conveyed by both Castaneda and Trungpa, magic has to do with overcoming the limitations of our ability to perceive beyond the ordinary limits of our subjective realities. Whether one is getting to other maps of reality, or learning to perceive an objective, primordial reality directly, the warrior's task is to overcome the limitations of his judgments, interpretations, and beliefs. There is a much bigger world out there than most of us think, and the only thing that keeps us from reaching it are the limitations our conditioning has placed on us. Perception, free of interpretation and fixed beliefs, is the gateway to magic.

Let us turn now to a related aspect of magic, which has to do with accessing powers or entities that lie beyond the ordinary realms. We have just seen that the drala energy can be viewed as an energy that descends, almost like an entity, to be tapped by the warrior.

In Castaneda's stories there are frequent encounters with beings called "allies," there is the peyote spirit "mescalito," and there is the gigantic, consciousness-devouring "eagle." Contact with any of them occurred only with a shift in state of consciousness. Sometimes the state shift resulted from power plants, sometimes from agitation of terror, sometimes from *stopping the world,* and sometimes from a strategically placed blow on the back by don Juan. In a sense, then, these were magical beings because they belonged to a description of reality different from what is possible in one's normal state. When Carlos shifted, they became perceivable; when he returned to normal, he usually doubted the validity of his experience because he could not reproduce it in his normal state of consciousness. When we read his books from the ordinary state of consciousness in our living rooms, Carlos' tales of encounters with the allies may be frightening to imagine, but they also seem far-fetched. Nevertheless, if you have been walking in the desert night for a couple of hours you are much more willing to believe such encounters are possible.

So, is one reality more true than another? Not necessarily. Knowledge needs to be refined and applied where it fits. The trick is not to get stuck believing that the possibilities of one perceptual position are valid across the board, or that they define "the truth."

Of the various themes of magic, we have found some commonality. Entering an altered state is necessary. In the new state there are different possibilities available. From any given state of consciousness some things are possible and some are not. Some things can be perceived and some cannot. Some things can be known and others cannot. In becoming fluid the warrior learns how to shift, and because he has this ability, more things are possible for him and more is available. This is related to his quest into the unknown in search of personal power. Having access to *the more,* the warrior receives more power as his relationship to the universe expands.

The ability to shift and to be fluid derives from discipline and impeccability. Discipline marshals the resources the warrior needs to become more and more impeccable. Becoming more impeccable, the warrior plugs power leaks and makes his power available for his quest into the unknown. By journeying into the unknown he broadens his relationship with the universe and gets even more power. Magic is his by the nature of the process. It becomes an ordinary part of the warrior's life and has nothing to do with superstition, and to the warrior, this magic has nothing to do with the occult because to him it is not hidden. Magic, remember, does not exist as a property of things or events. It exists as an attribution made in the mind of the beholder. The warrior knows about the state shifts that make magic possible and he knows that it is only magical from a point of view that cannot contain the event. By shifting point of view and by being fluid, the warrior experiences the so-called magical occurrence as a natural part of his expanded universe.

Will

To attain mastery a warrior must attain will. In the warriorship literature will is a major topic that never seems to receive a clear definition. The confusion over what will actually is stems from the fact that what is meant by will in the ordinary sense has little, if anything, to do with will as warriors manifest it.

Ouspensky points out in *The Fourth Way* that in ordinary parlance desire is mistaken for will.[4] This means that most people have no effective will at all, since their desires go in so many different directions at once. When you combine these various desires, having noticed that on one day one desire is prominent while on the next day a different desire is prominent, the effect is to cancel any particular direction and will is nowhere in evidence. Another way of talking about it is to say that ordinary people have many small wills, lasting only a short time, and that application of will in a comprehensive and consistent manner is impossible. That most people lack awareness of this process and believe in the illusion that they have will makes clarity on the subject even more difficult.

Ouspensky continues his discussion of will by saying that the will of a highly evolved person is singular rather than multiple and that it is based on three necessary components: knowledge, consciousness, and a permanent "I." Knowledge and consciousness are necessary acquisitions on the path to a permanent "I." In Chapter Six we saw that one's personality has many fragments, each masquerading as the real self. The advanced warrior has developed to the point that these small "I's" have become consolidated enough to give a more steady direction to his life. At the highest level, when a warrior is said to possess true will, there is only one will and only one "I." This true will belongs to one's essence, not to any personality fragment. Nevertheless, will is still a relative term and there are intermediate stages of development of will ranging from ordinary desires to true will. The warrior's task is to operate with the most mature will possible for his stage of growth. This means to struggle to free one's actions from mechanicalness and to escape slavery to one's likes and dislikes, desires and avoidances.

In Castaneda's writings, don Juan differentiates will from determination and courage. Will, he says, "is a kind of control ... a power within ourselves."[6] For don Juan, will is even more esoteric than for Ouspensky. Don Juan views will as a force linking men and the world and believes that one's will is instrumental, along with the senses, in forming our perceptions of the world.

Don Juan's way of explaining how the will can be used in such a way is to describe human beings as egg-shaped, luminous bundles of energy. Only people who know how to *see* can perceive them as such. In the place corresponding to the lower abdomen, there is a special spot in which the will lies. The energy from this spot below the navel can be extended out to apprehend and manipulate things in the world.

As with many of Castaneda's mystical tales, this explanation of the will as energy requires neither confirmation nor refutation to be useful. If it is accurate and one's path and predilection lead to the ability to *see* in this sense, the explanation will serve well. If will as energy is a metaphor, it still instructs us in the possibility of focusing our will so that we can apprehend and manipulate the world with it, or said differently, to influence our perceptions and affect the outcome of events.

Charles Tart touches briefly on the subject of will in *Waking Up*. In discussing approaches that develop the intelligence of the body and "instinctive intelligence" he says, "Developing the body/instinctive brain also leads to the development of a special kind of will power, one that does not depend on the push of strong emotional desire to win or brutish stubbornness, but on steadiness, skillfulness, and clarity of intent."[7] Here again, will is differentiated from the common ways in which it is conceived.

From these diverse points of view on will, it is difficult to give it a simple definition. Will is clearly stated to be something different from desires, determination, courage, and stubbornness. It is also clear from the writings that in ordinary circumstances most people do not possess will in any reliable and useful form, and that will must be developed along one's path. As a warrior's training and discipline take effect, will begins to form. To form it, one must strive to overcome mechanical action, thoughts, and feelings, and learn to live free of external restriction and inconsistent internal fluctuations.

As one's will grows, one can act with more consistency and integrity. Will enables the warrior to live strategically and become the master of himself. The development of will is intertwined with clarification of intent, acquisition of personal power, and unification of a permanent "I." Will might be said to be a combination of intent and personal power that can be used by one's total self to manifest intentions in the world. Developing will is worth the effort. As don Juan said, "Will is what can make you succeed when your thoughts tell you that you're defeated. Will is what makes you invulnerable."[8]

Detachment

An important attribute of warriors is detachment. It allows the warrior to move through the world with the flexibility necessary to change course when he should and the speed required to grasp his cubic centimeter of chance when it appears. With detachment the warrior can adopt the special type of anarchy that allows him to transect and exceed the boundaries delimited by the traditions of society and culture. In short, detachment keeps the warrior from getting stuck.

There are many arenas from which the warrior must seek detachment. An important one is detachment from outcome. Warriors are not on the side of either success or failure. Results inform the warrior about how closely his actions come to manifesting his intentions. The warrior's acts bring feedback and lack the emotional interpretations of success or failure. Being impeccable, the warrior does the best he can in all situations, but his efforts are made in the name of impeccability, not outcome. Since the warrior can "do," the outcome of his efforts is more likely to be in accord with his intention than not, but the warrior is still detached. His motivation comes from the process of his life, not a goal that is sought. Besides, we have learned from don Juan that "all paths are the same: they lead nowhere."[9] Ultimately we will all meet our fates—there is no point in getting attached to any particular desire for any certain outcome.

Allow me to illustrate this idea with a personal example. The value of detachment was eloquently communicated to me by a remarkable woman, Dr. Bonnie Vestal, who, as a pediatric oncologist, works with children involved with the ultimate question of outcome. After my father had been diagnosed with cancer Dr. Vestal told me his task was to attain peace of mind; it was not his task to survive. She advised that resolving unfinished business related to my father's personal, family, social, and spiritual issues would lead him to peace of mind, provided that he did not get attached to either life or death as an outcome. Desperately focusing on survival, warned Dr. Vestal, probably would result in a very painful, lingering illness, while focusing on peace would provide the best medium for his immune system to operate at maximum efficiency. Paradoxically, detachment, without abandoning oneself to one's death, seems to confer the highest probability of living. The focus, as in other aspects in a warrior's life, is to maximize the quality of the process of living while remaining detached from short-term or long-term outcomes.

Detachment from possessions is another important area to cultivate. Being attached to material possessions is like trying to set sail without weighing anchor. To be able to live with or without your possessions and to be equally fluid in either case is a major accomplishment for a warrior. It is also a very difficult accomplishment, but it must nevertheless be undertaken. Don Juan instructed Castaneda, "Your compulsion to possess and hold on to things is not unique. Everyone who wants to follow the warrior's path, the sorcerer's way, has to rid himself of this fixation."[10]

Possessions do not have to be material. One can relate to metaphysical concepts as if they are personal belongings. Trungpa cautioned, "Basic goodness can never become your personal possession. But you can invoke and provoke the uplifted energy of basic goodness in your life."[11] Such constructs as basic goodness, personal power, and impeccability are not possessions and are not unique to any individual. You can encounter them, cultivate them, invoke them, and use them, but you cannot own them.

Warriors also seek detachment from the trappings of identity. The roles one plays—brother, father, teacher, student, citizen—may be acted out by a warrior, but he does not adopt them as his identity. A warrior can engage in vocations and avocations fully, but he avoids attachment to and identification with them. Philosophies and belief systems, adopted without detachment, can be sources of a closed mind, no matter how elegant their structures. On the other end of the scale, people can attach to doubts, bewilderment, fears, and pain. Painful identities and grand ideas can be equally binding. Warriors gain a sense of detachment whether the object of attachment feels good or bad. The warrior also must detach from the opinions of other people. Trungpa tells of how warriors have abandoned gain, victory, and fame, and that as a warrior, "You are not dependent on feedback from others, because you have no doubt about yourself. You do not rely on encouragement or discouragement; therefore, you also have no need to display your valor to others."[12] To accept information from others without allowing their opinions to bind you, or to feel you have to impress them, is an ability the warrior acquires from detachment. The warrior's sense of worth does not come from the reference point of other people's opinions.

Relationships constitute another prime ground for attachment; therefore, the warrior relates to other people differently than what is usually done in the ordinary world. Detachment as a quality of a relationship does not mean the warrior lacks commitment to the person involved. On the contrary, when a warrior loves, he loves with his whole being. Still, the warrior does not demand that relationships remain static. He sees that they must be free to grow and change as the people in the relationship change. The pain is enormous when one person, in attempting to preserve the old form of a relationship, attempts to restrict growth and change in the other person. The warrior realizes that people grow, and because they do, relationships must grow too. When a relationship has outlived its usefulness to the people in it, the warrior will release it and let it go. On the other hand, if the relationship has continuing value for its participants, and if it must alter due to growth of the people in it, the warrior accepts that the relationship must change and it is likely that he too will change in the process. Such freedom requires a detached position.

Clearly, being detached does not mean being removed. Just as Gurdjieff's Fourth Way was designed to encourage the development of warriorship without having to sequester oneself in a monastery or hermitage, all warriors' paths maintain the warriors' contact with the world. Warriors will encounter and use all the objects of attachment mentioned above. The object is not to avoid possessions, relationships, or beliefs, but to deal with them in a detached way that does not restrict the warrior's advancement. Perhaps a better word would be *non-attachment,* meaning that you can be totally involved with something, but can release it and go on when necessary. This is the warrior's sense of detachment—to interact with the objects and people of the world, but remain non-attached.

To maintain a position of non-attachment the warrior must develop an extraordinarily high level of awareness and must combat identification. In doing so, the warrior gains the freedom and mobility that his path will require. He gains speed and perspective. Castaneda wrote that don Juan taught him that detachment "allowed the warrior to pause momentarily to reassess situations, to reconsider positions. In order to use that extra moment consistently and correctly, however, he said that a warrior had to struggle unyieldingly for a lifetime."[13]

The last three chapters have presented some major themes of a warrior's development. The warrior must come to terms with fear and learn fearlessness. He must cultivate a discipline to acquire skill and perseverance, then learn to relax within that discipline when necessary. He learns to change his state and shift his assemblage point to engage in magic, and expands his sensory abilities to contact the ordinary magic inherent in the world. The warrior cultivates his will by consolidating his personality fragments toward a central "I" so he can manifest his will in the world. Along the way he becomes free from the coercion of his likes and dislikes and can live strategically. This is done within a context of detachment that gives the warrior the fluidity needed to pursue his quest.

Chapter Twelve

The Open-Ended Conclusion

T his book attempts to outline and define warriorship in a way that gives it a form that is at once solid and mystical. In the source material the principles of warriorship are often very vague and it is difficult to determine exactly what the author had in mind in choosing his words. This is an excellent strategy for conveying a sense of mystery, and it leaves the reader free to make her own interpretations of the meaning of the ideas. All too often, however, the reader proceeds through the warrior book with a general feeling about the topics. By the end of the book one senses that something important and mystical has been discussed; but without enough explicit guidance, the reader does not follow through in applying the precepts of the book to her life. The warriorship material then remains an intriguing memory that hints at possibilities that never become actuality.

In these pages I have tried to cross-reference and compare various sources to provide some clarity regarding the aspects of warriorship. With that the reader can organize her thinking to produce action. The book seeks to provide a "big picture" of ideas such as personal power, impeccability, and the unknown so that specific practices in the source material make sense. With a more global understanding of what the conceptual language intends, the reader can set about finding the markers that distinguish her personal path with heart.

At the same time, I have tried to avoid setting these ideas in concrete. A large latitude of freedom for personal definition and interpretation remains. Many of the ideas become clear only when one engages in warrior practices and amasses personal experience along the way. It is beyond the scope of this book to formulate a complete compendium of warrior practices and to lay out a precisely engineered road of warriorship. The goal here is to provide a strategic outline with sufficient clarity that one may personally develop a path or can choose teachers or schools of warriorship practice, such as those provided by many of the authors of the source material. That being so, in this final chapter we will condense the essentials into a more concise outline and end with some hints about what lies beyond warriorship itself.

The Origins

The term "warrior" applies because strategic practices and approaches to maximizing one's capacities to live life have come down from ancient warrior traditions. Those warriors knew that survival in battle depended on being radically present in the here and now, maintaining acute awareness of themselves and their surroundings, and acting with their full capacities. The ancient warriors' approaches can be transposed to modern times so that contemporary people have tools to maximize the quality of life, have a code that guides their decisions, and have a context in which their acts have purpose and meaning. Therefore, the term warrior itself is a metaphor for a way of living that maximizes one's resources and personal power and provides a strategic blueprint for self-organization. Consequently, it is possible to make sense of Millman's term "peaceful warrior" and avoid any necessity to live in a bellicose manner. "War" and "battle" are metaphors because survival, if not of vital signs, then certainly of quality of life, is at issue for everyone. We have this life to live and, as we have learned, we can choose to live like slaves or like warriors.

The Definition

A warrior is an impeccable hunter of personal power. You will recall that personal power is that "stuff" or "energy" or "process" that provides our life force and gives us the ability *to do.* Perhaps it is the life force itself. Our relationship with the universe confers this power and we all have some of it, as evidenced by our being alive. The important question is, how alive do you want to be? To feel more alive, one must expand one's relationship with the universe, which is the way to acquire more personal power. This expanded relationship with the universe means that the warrior has more knowledge than before and has greater capacity for effectiveness. It has often been said that knowledge is power and this is especially true for the warrior because she translates knowledge into productive action. This reflects Feldenkrais' assertion that thinking means new ways of acting. The path with heart entails *doing* and the warrior continually seeks to improve her ability *to do*.

The Known, The Unknown and Personal Power

To understand how to expand one's relationship with the universe, warriors distinguish between the known and the unknown. The greater one's domain of the known, the more effective one can be and the more one can *do*. Therefore, it is necessary to expand the known by delving into that realm of infinite proportions, the unknown. Only by forays into the unknown can warriors grasp new knowledge. If the size of one's known stays the same, no new capacities or possibilities can develop and there is no increase in personal power. This is the road to stagnation and senility.

Ah, but the unknown is the limitless storehouse of possibilities. All knowledge, all ideas, all abilities beyond what one currently has are in the unknown. It is, therefore, the lair of personal power, and the warrior must journey there to harvest knowledge and transform it into power. It is in this quest that the warrior must depart from living the ordinary life, for journeying into the unknown is minimized in ordinary life. To go beyond the limits of the known requires great personal power already. Accordingly, the warrior must marshal her personal power to cross the border into the unknown, and she does so by the process of saving the power she already has, not letting it leak away and be wasted. This process is called impeccability and it forms the frame around much of the warrior's discipline, practices, and decisions.

Impeccability

Impeccability is the process of plugging power leaks so that personal power does not drain away into useless pursuits. The warrior has better use for her initial ration of personal power—she needs it to enter the unknown, survive the journey, and convert knowledge into the ability *to do.* There are numerous power leaks, such as self-importance, identification, binding habits, uncontrolled imagination, and negative emotions. The warrior's discipline and specific practices enable her to plug those leaks and apply the saved personal power to her quest.

There are a few universal considerations in developing impeccability, besides doing specific practices. A tool that is essential in plugging all power leaks is awareness, for without awareness a warrior is blind to the times and ways in which she loses power. Another tool is the disruption of routines and habits. After becoming aware of a habit one can intentionally disrupt it or the circumstances in which she exercises the habit. Thus, much power is freed. Perhaps it is more accurate to speak of habits as power "sinks" than power leaks because they tend to bind power instead of dispersing it. Habitual thinking patterns, emotional responses, perceptual modes, and actions all require energy to maintain. The trap is that habits feel familiar and we mistake familiarity for lack of effort. Thus, we do not realize the tremendous energy bound up in our habits unless we somehow experience what it feels like *not* to do the habit. The contrast illuminates the amount of power expended in maintaining our various habits and routines. Warriors seek to disrupt routines and free themselves from the power sink of habits to make that power available for the quest into the unknown. Beyond these general considerations there is a wide array of specific practices a warrior can use to pursue impeccability. It is important to realize that perfect impeccability probably will be a goal that remains forever elusive. Nevertheless, impeccability improves by degrees and each degree frees personal power for the warrior's productive use.

Pursuing impeccability requires discipline, and we use this word in two ways. One way refers to the gumption to stay on the path, to apply awareness, and to maintain specific practices for plugging power leaks. The other way refers to specific disciplined practices, such as meditation. This kind of discipline hones the warrior's innate capacities, synchronizing body, mind, and spirit. It is a way of tuning one's instrument in preparation for the symphony of the warrior's life.

Discipline relates to impeccability but also can be a vehicle into the unknown. Meditation and esoteric spiritual practices can carry one far from the known and provide glimpses into unknown realms. Also spanning the gap between impeccability in the known domain and the mysteries of the unknown is the warrior's way of dealing with fear. Fear, allied to lack of personal power, is the primary barrier to the unknown. The warrior is free to experience fear but must not let fear control her. She must face her fear, evaluate it, and if she has the power, move beyond it. She cannot let fear hijack her and render her immobile. If, in evaluating her fear, the warrior learns that she is involved in something beyond her ability to handle, she retreats long enough to develop the necessary power. The retreat is based on her assessment, intuitively or rationally determined, that she needs more capacity. She does not retreat simply because she is afraid. This is part of a strategic process of exploring the unknown without going so deep that disaster occurs.

Warriors' Epistemology

The unknown itself presents a dilemma when talking about it. In Taoist tradition the tao that can be spoken is not the eternal Tao, and speaking of the unknown puts us in a similar bind. It is impossible to describe the ineffable, so our discussions must be limited to establishing that the unknown is somehow different from the known and to the processes by which the known is sculpted from the raw material of the unknown.

The first consideration is to recognize that the known world is, in the epistemology of warriors, a description and not a hard fact. It is an invention, not a discovery. Out of the great cosmic soup of the unknown, through language and thought, we condense certain elements into what we treat as reality. NLP and cybernetics say that the map is not the territory. Even so, in ordinary life people treat their maps as if that were the only possible reality and go to tremendous lengths and efforts to preserve that illusion. The warrior, on the other hand, becomes both a cartographer and a collector of maps. She realizes that reality can be constructed in various ways and she seeks to alter her descriptions and attain the flexibility to use a variety of maps, according to her purpose at the time. This is the context in which the warrior seeks to *stop the world.* In suspending her customary description of reality, she gains access to alternate realities. If the warrior were to insist that reality remain constant, she would never explore beyond the boundaries of the known. For returning from the unknown and retrieving new knowledge entails an expansion beyond the old known. Elements of reality from before may carry over into the new reality, but the shape of reality and the location of its boundaries will be forever different. The known, to the warrior, is forever changing and she can suspend her description to get to the unknown, gather new knowledge, and return to a reconstructed reality in which she has greater personal power.

The Frontier

Crossing the border into the unknown is always a test of the warrior's training and skill. Confusion and fear usually accompany warrior and common man alike in crossing the frontier, but how people act after that is the key. The ordinary person is likely to be frozen with fear, to be blinded by confusion, and to retreat. The warrior has a momentous skill in that she knows what to do when she does not know what to do. As in the rest of her life, the warrior responds strategically to the situation. Her strategy includes the following elements:

1. Recognizing that the feelings of confusion and panic mean that she has crossed the frontier. The warrior does not indulge in the feelings, but moves beyond them.
2. Shifting to higher levels of awareness of self and surroundings. She gathers information about the new situation, instead of relying on old data from the known.
3. Relying on internal rather than external reference points, realizing that familiar external landmarks do not exist in the unknown.
4. Not-doing of habitual responses. New circumstances call for flexibility and choice.

Knowing what to do when you don't know what to do allows you to journey into the unknown, use expanded perception to enhance your relationship with the universe, and return to the known claiming knowledge as power.

The warrior's particular path often determines where she crosses into the unknown. Castaneda spoke of the warrior finding and following her *path with heart,* which means taking a direction that gives meaning and purpose to one's life. A person is, of course, free to select any path, and all paths ultimately lead to the same end anyway— death. So, it is really a question of how one wants to live. The path with heart makes life a source of joy and bliss. It serves to strengthen the traveller rather than weaken her. It is not always a bed of roses, and having the discipline to stay on the path is not always easy. It takes much personal power. It takes fortitude to stay with the path because one cannot see very far ahead. Since the path winds in and out of the unknown, unpredictable changes will occur. Still, the warrior's discipline prepares her to deal with the expected and the unexpected with equal facility.

The Warrior's Anarchy

Another source of difficulty can be that other people often put up roadblocks to the traveller of the path with heart. Social norms and institutions are designed to preserve the status quo, and paths with heart have a way of leading to new territory and new actions. The warrior cannot be a warrior if she abandons or reroutes her path because she is stepping outside convention and the cubbyholes that the social order dictates. The warrior seeks breakthroughs, deliberately invoking alternate realities, alternate descriptions, and other ways of viewing the world. This makes the warrior an anarchist and a revolutionary, but not a delinquent or rebel. The warrior makes her choices regarding social institutions based on her strategy for living and questing for personal power. The delinquent is merely defiant. The revolutionary discovers new paradigms, the rebel just fights with old ones. It is not that the warrior is deliberately anti-social, it is that she does not let artificial social prescriptions and proscriptions deter her explorations. She does so with much preparation, thought, and responsibility. The warrior's brand of anarchy requires impeccability.

The warrior mythology outlines a code for living. It is a way of living a life of increasing effectiveness, seeking new knowledge and capabilities, expanding one's relationship with the universe. The warrior seeks impeccability through the plugging of power leaks and disruption of routines. Then she uses the saved power to hunt even more power by questing in the unknown. To do this the warrior must lead a disciplined, strategic life. She must come to terms with fear, know what to do when she doesn't know what to do, and employ a special form of anarchy that frees her from compliance with the status quo. This road is challenging and it does not appeal to everyone. The warrior's path is a process, not a destination or outcome. As long as one is on the path, one is a warrior, regardless if she is at a beginning, intermediate, or advanced level.

Beyond Warriorship

For some, the warrior's way is sufficient, a process that is an end in itself. But, does something lie beyond it? In Castaneda's terms living like a warrior was necessary preparation for becoming a *man of knowledge.* This ultimately entailed the ability to take one's acquired awareness into another realm permanently. It involved being fluent in a variety of radically different realities and it involved *seeing. Seeing* in this sense involved the ability to look beyond the ordinary, material appearance of things and fathom the energetic nature behind the material level.

In our earlier discussion of quantum mechanics we noted that realities are created by an act of observation, and we related that to the process of description that other sources say creates realities. The act of observing, in the scientific speculations, led to collapsing a mathematical structure called a wave, or probability, function. In this view the nature of the universe is mathematical, a disembodied wave of probability in which possible realities have different likelihoods of becoming manifest. By the interaction with an observer the probability wave collapses and the observer encounters a certainty. At that moment she observes one particular reality and no others because the probability of the others falls to zero percent. But is it possible to apprehend or comprehend the wave itself?

Castaneda spoke of a complex system of emanations and how we have an assemblage point that allows us to perceive only certain bands of emanations at a time. When our assemblage point is in certain positions we can perceive certain kinds of realities and not others. The warrior uses her personal power to shift her assemblage point in conjunction with stopping the world. This corresponds with collapsing the wave function at certain points on its curve and making an apparent, virtual reality. Another way of saying this is that the position of the assemblage point determines what maps the warrior can draw at any particular time.

We have said earlier that the warrior's epistemology holds that the map is not the territory and that we make our maps (realities, worlds) by acts of description that determine what we can perceive and what we cannot. The warrior's way teaches us how to draw a variety of maps, giving us tremendous flexibility. But might it be possible to view the territory directly? This ability would be beyond warriorship, but living like a warrior would be necessary to generate the tremendous amount of personal power it would take to bypass maps altogether and apprehend the territory itself.

Now we are again in the realm of the Tao that cannot be spoken. This is the province beyond words, beyond description, beyond thought, beyond the intellect's powers. It is the realm of mystical practice, not of reason. Buddhism speaks of the unconditional nature of reality, the nature that exists before thought discriminates form. Apprehending the territory entails not stopping the world to let an alternate reality form, but stopping the world and finding out what happens when we do not form another reality with another description. The world stops and we do not construct another map. We remain accessible to whatever it is that we represent with our maps—the Buddhists' unconditional nature. In this state there is no subject-object duality. There is a unitive consciousness in which all things totally interconnect and resonate.

This unitive state of consciousness can occur when the sense of boundaries between "me" and "not me" become blurred or permeable, such as in intense states of love, creativity, ecstasy, empathy, or under influences of drugs or other processes affecting brain chemistry. They also ensue from meditative spiritual practices.

Practitioners of many religions have reported this kind of experience: the Cabalists of Judaism, Sufis of Islam, shaman of the so-called pagan religions, yogis of Hindu religions, monks of Buddhism and Taoism, and various monastics and saints of Christianity. Note that these examples involve mystical or meditative practices rather than the cognitive following of a religious dogma. In these practices, the practitioner communes with the spiritual, divine, or metaphysical realm directly, without intercession of priesthood or clergy. It is a direct experience and a journey that is a product of personal discipline and personal power.

Warriorship, then, is a code of living that enhances one's effectiveness in life by expanding the relationship with the universe and gathering more personal power by transforming knowledge into power through action. The warrior develops her being and her knowledge. This alone gives the means to escape from what Gurdjieff called the prison of ordinary life. The warrior's way is open to anyone with the spunk to try it. Beyond warriorship are even more liberating experiences, but these require the power not only to move past the limitations that exist in the prison of ordinary life, but to gain relationship with the mystical, unconditioned nature that is beyond what can be described. The warrior's way can give you that power.

Appendix

Training and Information

1. Robert Spencer offers a variety of experientially-based workshops on the themes of this book. Contact him by writing to the following address:

> Robert Spencer
> 4112 South Chicago Avenue
> Nampa, Idaho 83686

2. For information about the Feldenkrais Method, Feldenkrais Teachers, Teacher training courses, or the works of Moshe Feldenkrais contact:

> The Feldenkrais Guild®
> 524 Ellsworth Street
> P.O. Box 489
> Albany, Oregon 97321-0143
> (800) 775-2118, Fax (503) 926-0572

3. Another source of books, audiotapes, and videotapes of the works of Moshe Feldenkrais and other Feldenkrais Practitioners is:

> Feldenkrais Resources
> P.O. Box 2067
> Berkeley, California 94201
> (800) 765-1907

4. Dan Millman offers trainings, seminars, audiotapes, and other services. Contact:

> Peaceful Warrior Services
> P.O. Box 6148—Dept. NOM
> San Rafael, California 94903
> (415) 491-0301

5. There are Shambhala Training Centers throughout North America and Europe. For information contact:

> Shambhala Training International
> 1084 Tower Road
> Halifax MS B3H 2Y5,
> Canada
> (902) 423-3266

6. Nelson Zink offers training and experience in many of the ideas and practices presented in *The Structure of Delight.* Contact:

> Nelson Zink
> P.O. Box 68
> Embudo, New Mexico 87531
> (505) 579-4329

7. For information about NLP and practitioner training, contact:

> International Association of Neuro-Linguistic Programming
> 342 Massachusetts Avenue
> 200 Marott Center
> Indianapolis, Indiana 46204
> (317) 663-6059

8. To find out about training in the Trager Method, contact:

> The Trager Institute
> 33 Millwood
> Mill Valley, California 94941
> (415) 388-2688

9. For information about The Alexander Technique, write or call:

> The North American Society of Teachers of The Alexander Technique
> P.O. Box 3992
> Champaign, Illinois 61826
> (800) 473-0620

10. Information about Eutony is available from:
    Joyce Riveros-Olivarez
    International Center for Mind-Body Studies
    1633 Julian Drive
    El Cerrito, California 94530
    (510) 234-9362

11. For information about Iyengar Yoga contact:
    Iyengar Yoga Institute of San Francisco
    2404 27th Avenue
    San Francisco, California 94116
    (415) 753-0909

Chapter Notes

Chapter One

1. Carlos Castaneda, *A Separate Reality* (New York: Simon and Schuster, 1971), 150.
2. Chögyam Trungpa, *Shambhala, The Sacred Path of the Warrior* (New York: Bantam, 1986), 7.
3. Georges Ivanovitch Gurdjieff, *Life Is Real Only Then, When "I Am"*, Frontisepiece (New York: Viking Penguin, 1991).
4. *Ibid.*
5. *Ibid.*
6. Alfred Korzybski, *Science and Sanity* (New York: Science Press, 1941). See also Gregory Bateson, *Steps to an Ecology of Mind* (New York: Chandler, 1972), 180.

Chapter Two

1. Carlos Castaneda, *The Teachings of Don Juan, A Yaqui Way of Knowledge* (New York: Simon and Schuster, 1975), 150.
2. Castaneda, *A Separate Reality*, 218.
3. Dan Millman, *Way of the Peaceful Warrior* (Tiburon, CA: H. J. Kramer, 1984), 48.
4. Carlos Castaneda, *The Fire from Within* (New York: Simon and Schuster, 1984), 152.
5. Carlos Castaneda, *The Eagle's Gift* (New York: Simon and Schuster, 1981), 281.
6. Carlos Castaneda, *Journey to Ixtlan* (New York: Simon and Schuster, 1972), 83.
7. Dennis Leri, Editor's Page in *The Feldenkrais Journal, Issue Number 2.* (San Francisco: The Feldenkrais Guild, 1986), 2.

8. Trungpa, *Shambhala,* 32.
9. Carlos Castaneda, *Tales of Power* (New York: Simon and Schuster, 1976), 196.
10. Trungpa, *Shambhala,* 25.
11. Castaneda, *The Fire from Within,* 240.
12. Trungpa, *Shambhala,* 15.
13. Castaneda, *Tales of Power,* 75.
14. Millman, *Way of the Peaceful Warrior,* 191.
15. Trungpa, *Shambhala,* 39.
16. Castaneda, *Tales of Power,* 105.
17. Trungpa, *Shambhala,* 41.
18. Carlos Castaneda, *The Second Ring of Power* (New York: Simon and Schuster, 1977), 271.
19. Nelson Zink, *The Structure of Delight* (Taos: Mind Matters, 1991), 195.
20. *Ibid.,* 233.
21. Robert S. deRopp, *Warrior's Way, The Challenging Life Games* (New York: Delacorte Press, 1979), 208.
22. Castaneda, *Journey To Ixtlan,* 234.
23. Castaneda, *The Fire from Within,* 179.
24. Castaneda, *The Eagle's Gift,* 308.
25. Castaneda, *A Separate Reality,* 133.
26. Dennis Leri, "Dreams in the Warrior's Wake" in *The Feldenkrais Journal,* #2 (San Francisco: The Feldenkrais Guild, 1986), 37.
27. Trungpa, *Shambhala,* 102.
28. *Ibid.,* 73.
29. DeRopp, *Warrior's Way,* 102.
30. Millman, *Way of the Peaceful Warrior,* 183.

Chapter Three

1. Millman, *Way of the Peaceful Warrior,* 186.
2. Lawrence LeShan, *How to Meditate,* (New York: Bantam, 1984).
3. Trungpa, *Shambhala,* 77.
4. Castaneda, *The Eagle's Gift,* 35.
5. Castaneda, *The Second Ring of Power,* 123.
6. *Ibid.,* 170.

7. Castaneda, *The Fire from Within*, 109.
8. *Ibid.*, 69.

Chapter Four

1. Castaneda, *The Fire from Within*, 88.
2. Trungpa, *Shambhala*, 91.
3. *Ibid.*
4. *Ibid.*, 96.
5. Millman, *Way of the Peaceful Warrior*, 31.
6. *Ibid.*, 134.
7. *Ibid.*, 112.
8. Jean Houston, "The Possible Human Workshop," Salt Lake City, 1982.
9. Zink, *The Structure of Delight*, 63.
10. *Ibid.*, 180.
11. Robert Dilts, Tim Hallbom, and Suzi Smith, *Beliefs, Pathways to Health & Well Being*, (Portland, OR: Metamorphous Press, 1991), 43.
12. Zink, *The Structure of Delight*, 73.
13. Castaneda, *Tales of Power*, 107.

Chapter Five

1. Castaneda, *The Fire from Within*, 26, 29.
2. Carlos Castaneda, *The Power of Silence*, (New York: Simon and Schuster, 1987), 171.
3. Trungpa, *Shambhala*, 25.
4. Castaneda, *Tales of Power*, 174.
5. *Ibid.*, 19.
6. Trungpa, *Shambhala*, 18.
7. Castaneda, *The Eagle's Gift*, 281.
8. Castaneda, *Journey to Ixtlan*, 121.
9. Castaneda, *The Fire from Within*, 33.
10. Castaneda, *Journey to Ixtlan*, 120.

Chapter Six

1. Charles T. Tart, *Waking Up, Overcoming the Obstacles to*

Human Potential, (Boston: Shambhala Publications, 1986), 109.

2. J. G. Bennett, *Transformation*, (Charles Town, WVa: Claymont Communications, 1978), 36.

3. P. D. Ouspensky, *The Fourth Way*, (New York: Vintage Books, 1971), 124.

4. Dan Millman, *The Warrior Athlete*, (Walpole, NH: Stillpoint Publishing, 1979), 21.

5. Ouspensky, *The Fourth Way*, 124.

6. *Ibid.*, 56.

7. Tart, *Waking Up*, 197.

8. *Ibid.*, 124.

9. *Ibid.*, 201.

10. Ouspensky, *The Fourth Way*, 10.

11. Millman, *The Warrior Athlete*, 67–69.

12. *Ibid.*

13. Millman, *Way of the Peaceful Warrior*, 131.

14. Millman, *The Warrior Athlete*, 64.

15. Millman, *Way of the Peaceful Warrior*, 62.

16. *Ibid.*, 81.

17. Ouspensky, *The Fourth Way*, 73.

18. Millman, *Way of the Peaceful Warrior*, 113.

19. Dan Millman, *No Ordinary Moments*, (Tiburon, CA: H. J. Kramer, 1992), 273.

20. Ouspensky, *The Fourth Way*, 9.

21. Moshe Feldenkrais, *Amherst Training Videotapes*, The Feldenkrais Guild.

22. Ouspensky, *The Fourth Way*, 62.

23. Leri, "Dreams in the Warrior's Wake", 37.

24. Tart, *Waking Up*, 229.

25. *Ibid.*, 230.

26. Castaneda, *Tales of Power*, 19.

27. *Ibid.*, 289.

28. Michael Murphy, *Golf in the Kingdom*, (New York: Viking Press, 1972), III.

Chapter Seven

1. Castaneda, *The Eagle's Gift*, 281.
2. Castaneda, *The Fire from Within*, 46.
3. Ken Wilbur, *The Holographic Paradigm and Other Paradoxes*, (Boulder: Shambhala Publications, 1982), 64.
4. Castaneda, *Tales of Power*, 125, 126.
5. *Ibid.*, 126.
6. Gary Zukav, *The Dancing Wu Li Masters, An Overview of the New Physics*, (New York: Bantam, 1979), 85.
7. Castaneda, *The Fire from Within*, 55.
8. *Ibid.*, 50.
9. *Ibid.*, 152.

Chapter Eight

1. Leri, "Dreams In The Warrior's Wake", 36.
2. *Webster's Seventh New Collegiate Dictionary*, (Springfield, MA: Merriam, 1976), 666.

Chapter Nine

1. Frank Herbert, *Dune*, (New York: Putnam, 1984), 8.
2. Trungpa, *Shambhala*, 21.
3. *Ibid.*
4. *Ibid.*, 29.
5. *Ibid.*, 27.
6. *Ibid.*, 12.
7. *Ibid.*, 52.
8. *Ibid.*, 37.
9. *Ibid.*, 35.
10. *Ibid.*, 39.
11. Millman, *Way of the Peaceful Warrior*, 62.
12. Millman, *The Warrior Athlete*, 68.
13. *Ibid.*, 67.
14. *Ibid.*
15. Millman, *Way of the Peaceful Warrior*, 170–172.
16. *Ibid.*, 133.

17. Castaneda, *The Teachings of Don Juan*, 197.
18. Castaneda, *Tales of Power*, 27.
19. Castaneda, *The Fire from Within*, 240.
20. Tart, *Waking Up*, 242.
21. Judith DeLozier and John Grinder, *Turtles All The Way Down*, (Bonny Doon, CA: Grinder, DeLozier and Associates, 1987), 69–71.
22. *Ibid.,* 164.
23. Leslie Cameron-Bandler and Michael Lebeau, *The Emotional Hostage*, (San Rafael, CA: Futurepace, Inc., 1986), 35,36.
24. *Ibid.,* 212.

Chapter Ten

1. Jeremy W. Hayward, *Perceiving Ordinary Magic: Science and Intuitive Wisdom,* (Boston: Shambhala Publications, 1984), 18.
2. Millman, *Way of The Peaceful Warrior*, 92.
3. Hayward, *Perceiving Ordinary Magic*, 261.
4. *Ibid.,* 271.
5. *Ibid.,* 270.
6. *Ibid.*
7. Thomas Hanna, *The Body of Life* (New York: Alfred A. Knopf, 1980).
8. Silva Mehta, Mira Mehta, and Shyam Mehta, *Yoga the Iyengar Way,* (New York: Alfred A. Knopf, 1990), 8.
9. *Ibid.,* 173.
10. *Ibid.,* 164.
11. *Ibid.*
12. *Ibid.*
13. David Bersin, "An Interview With Gerda Alexander", in *Somatics,* Autumn/Winter 1983–84: 4.
14. *Ibid.,* 7.
15. *Ibid.*
16. Trungpa, *Shambhala*, 56.
17. Murphy, *Golf in the Kingdom*, 194.

Chapter Eleven

1. Hayward, *Perceiving Ordinary Magic*, 258.
2. Trungpa, *Shambhala*, 80.
3. *Ibid.*, 83–85.
4. Ouspensky, *The Fourth Way*, 252.
5. Castaneda, *A Separate Reality*, 146, 147.
6. Tart, *Waking Up*, 153.
7. Castaneda, *A Separate Reality*, 146.
8. Castaneda, *The Teachings of Don Juan*, 107.
9. Castaneda, *The Eagle's Gift*, 28.
10. Trungpa, *Shambhala*, 61.
11. *Ibid.*, 136.
12. Castaneda, *The Eagle's Gift*, 117.

Index

Index